Selecting a
College Major

Selecting a College Major

Exploration and Decision Making

Fifth Edition

Virginia N. Gordon, Ph.D.
Susan J. Sears, Ph.D.
The Ohio State University

PEARSON

Prentice
Hall

Upper Saddle River, New Jersey
Columbus, Ohio

Library of Congress Cataloging in Publication Data

Gordon, Virginia N.
    Selecting a college major: exploration and decision making / Virginia N. Gordon, Susan
  J. Sears.--5th ed.
      p. cm.
    Rev. ed. of: Academic alternatives. 4th ed. c1997.
    ISBN 0-13-039585-4 (pbk.)
    1. College majors. I. Sears, Susan Jones II. Title.

LB2361.G67 2004

2002044451

Vice President and Publisher: Jeffery W. Johnston
Senior Acquisitions Editor: Sande Johnson
Assistant Editor: Cecilia Johnson
Production Editor: JoEllen Gohr
Production Coordination: Carlisle Publishers Services
Design Coordinator: Diane C. Lorenzo
Cover Designer: Jeff Vanik
Cover Image: SuperStock
Production Manager: Pamela D. Bennett
Director of Marketing: Ann Castel Davis
Director of Advertising: Kevin Flanagan
Marketing Manager: Christina Quadhamer

This book was set in Times by Carlisle Communications, Ltd. It was printed and bound by Banta Book Group. The cover was printed by Phoenix Color Corp.

Previous editions, entitled *Academic Alternatives: Exploration and Decision Making,* copyright © 1992, 1997 by Gorsuch Scarisbrick, Publishers.

Pearson Education Ltd.
Pearson Education Singapore Pte. Ltd.
Pearson Education Canada, Ltd.
Pearson Education—Japan

Pearson Education Australia Pty. Limited,
Pearson Education North Asia Ltd.
Pearson Educación de Mexico, S.A. de C.V.
Pearson Education Malaysia Pte. Ltd.

10 9 8 7 6 5 4 3 2 1
ISBN 0-13-039585-4

Dedication

This book is dedicated to all the students who have been undecided about a college major and who have faced the challenge of deciding with fortitude and courage.

Brief Contents

Contents

Unit Three   Exploring Majors   29

Unit Four   Exploring Occupations   57

Unit Five   Making a Decision   73

Preface

Choosing a college major can be a difficult and sometimes confusing decision for many students. First-year college students, in particular, have little experience with many of the academic disciplines represented in college curricula. They have limited understanding of how knowledge is "artificially" divided into smaller units or disciplines and how the sum of this knowledge is interrelated and intertwined.

Many entering students have only a vague idea of what a "major" entails, not only in the coursework required, but in its real-life applications in the work world. Some students wrongly perceive that their choice of major leads directly to a "job."

With the bewildering array of educational and career options available today, many students choose to be "undecided" when they enter college. They recognize the advantage of exploring the academic options open to them on their campus. This workbook is designed to assist them in this information-gathering and deciding process.

Often students want or need to change the major they initially chose. Some change for personal reasons, such as a lack of interest in the subject matter or exposure to other academic areas that lead to new interests. Some students cannot retain their initial choice of major because of their inability to perform academically at a certain level in the required coursework. This problem, in addition to the limited number of applicants taken into some selective or oversubscribed majors, creates a situation that forces students to choose other majors.

Advanced students who are rethinking an earlier choice might be somewhat constrained by their earned academic credit that may not be viable for some of the alternative majors they are considering. Students who are in the process of changing majors need the type of academic advising that can help them integrate previous course credit into new directions. Up until now, there has been no publication to help this large (and sometimes unrecognized or unacknowledged) group of students explore other choices in a systematic way. This workbook has been developed to assist not only the "undecided" student with selecting a major, but also the "major-changer" who is exploring alternative options.

Unit One encourages students to review their current academic situation and helps them assess their method for approaching and making decisions, both past and present. Unit Two involves students in self-assessment and helps them consider their personal strengths and limitations. Unit Three is concerned with identifying and exploring various academic major options from three perspectives. Students select several realistic majors and collect detailed information about them.

Once these academic areas have been identified, students explore related occupational fields in Unit Four. Unit Five helps them narrow down alternatives so that appropriate academic planning can take place. Developing an academic graduation plan helps students summarize all they have learned into a practical vehicle for future planning and implementation. Unit Six guides students in implementing their academic major decision. The appendix offers an optional opportunity for students who are interested in developing their resume writing and job searching skills.

This workbook leads students through an orderly, rational approach to selecting a college major. Not only are students encouraged to gather detailed educational and career information, but they are also encouraged to identify their feelings about the process as they are experiencing it. The authors hope this combination of cognitive and affective searching will lead to satisfying, long-term, realistic educational decisions.

This new edition reflects the incredible technological advancement of the Internet, which provides the information resources that are so important in educational and occupational decision making. Internet resources include those for assessing one's personal interests, abilities, and values; information about myriad educational options; and (perhaps the most extensive) information resources for exploring occupational fields that have direct or indirect connections to academic areas. Many of the assignments in this workbook require students to access the Internet for this information.

The authors wish to thank George Steele, Melinda McDonald, Deb Serling, and Tracy Tupman, whose understanding and sensitivity to these types of college students provided many insights into the approaches used in this workbook. For sharing their expertise with us as reviewers of this new edition, special thanks to Jackie Balzer, Oregon State University; Pamela Church, Skagit Valley College; Ann Hein, University of Nevada, Las Vegas; Deborah McCoy, University of California–Riverside; Elisabeth Meyer, SUNY Brockport; Allyson Tanouye, University of Hawaii at Manoa; and Kathleen Thayer, Purdue University.

Introduction

*The individual becomes conscious of himself as being this particular
individual with particular gifts, tendencies, impulses, passions, under the
influence of a particular product of his milieu. He who becomes thus
conscious of himself assumes all this as part of his own responsibility. At the
moment of choice he is in complete isolation, for he withdraws from his
surroundings; and he is in complete continuity, for he chooses himself as
product; and this choice is a free choice, so that we might even say, when he
chooses himself as product, that he is producing himself.*

—Søren Kierkegaard

One of the first important decisions you face when you enter college is the choice of
an area of study. Some students are very certain about their choice of college major,
some are tentatively decided but have some doubts, some have narrowed their options
to two or three, and some are totally undecided. Regardless of the decision level you
initially experience, you need some time to either confirm your choice or explore academic alternatives. The process of confirmation or exploration needs to involve you
in the gathering and integration of information. If you are exploring, you need to be
involved in learning not only about the possible majors at your institution and what
coursework is required, but also about how specific majors relate to your personal
characteristics and career goals.

You may be a student who has found that after you have made a choice of major,
your plans are thwarted. Perhaps your initial choice was not realistic or attainable,
based on your own changing interests or abilities, or the institution's policies about
selective or oversubscribed majors. It is critical for you as a major-changer to examine your personal strengths in a new light and to identify new majors that will satisfy
your changing academic and career goals.

This workbook helps you move through a process of logical steps that lead to a
major and perhaps a career decision. These steps are outlined in the model displayed
in Figure 1 on the next page. While these steps are progressive, the process should be
considered fluid. That is, the results of one step may indicate a need to return to a previous step if the desired outcome is not possible. For example, you may find that the
course requirements in a major that appears interesting do not match your academic
aptitudes and strengths. In this case, you might need to return to the "exploring majors" step to gather new or additional information. Or you may have made a commitment to a selective major but find you cannot enter it because you are unable to meet
the criteria established by that academic department. You may need to return to the
"information gathering" step in order to identify alternative academic majors that will
match your proven abilities, accept much of the coursework you have already taken,
and relate to general career areas you consider attractive.

As you confirm or explore academic alternatives, keep an open mind for viewing
information in an unbiased light. Also, be willing to work hard and be dedicated to see-
ing the task to completion. Although the decision about an academic major is not a sim-
ple one, the rewards for selecting a major that is realistic and satisfying will become
apparent over a period of time. Through the activities, discussions, and assignments in

this course, you will be setting important academic and career goals and creating a plan that will help you move toward graduation.

At the end of every unit in this book, you will be asked to discuss case studies of students who are making the same kinds of decisions you are making. Each case study illustrates a step of the process outlined in the model in Figure 1. You will also be asked to keep a log to help you reflect and summarize what you have learned about yourself at each step of the way.

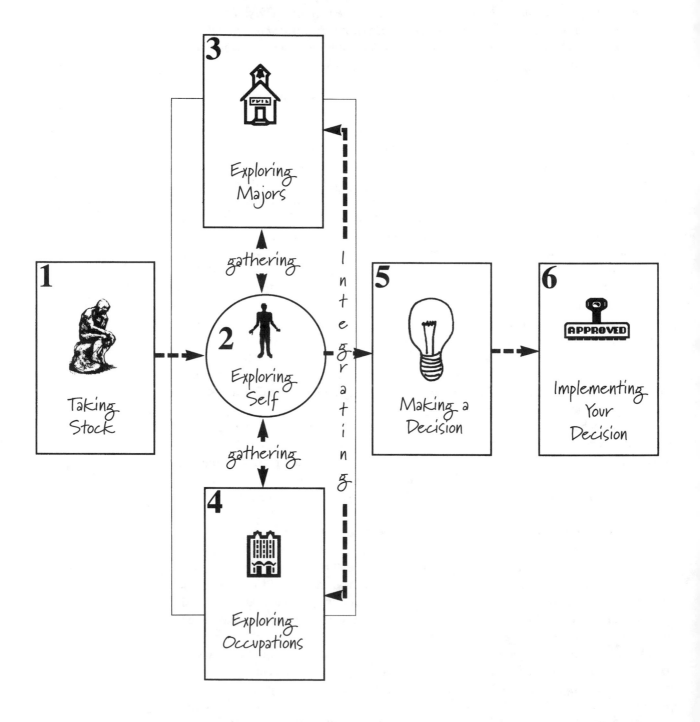

Figure 1. Model for academic exploration and decision making.

Selecting a College Major

UNIT ONE
Taking Stock

IN THIS UNIT, you will take stock of your current situation and examine how it has resulted in your decision either to be undecided about your major or to change it. This reflection will help you realistically evaluate past and present decisions and give you a foundation for exploring academic and career alternatives.

Taking stock is not always easy. It may involve looking at some frustrating or painful decisions you made in the past or at your inability to make a decision. Taking stock is vital, however, if you are to move on to the next step in exploring possible academic and career directions.

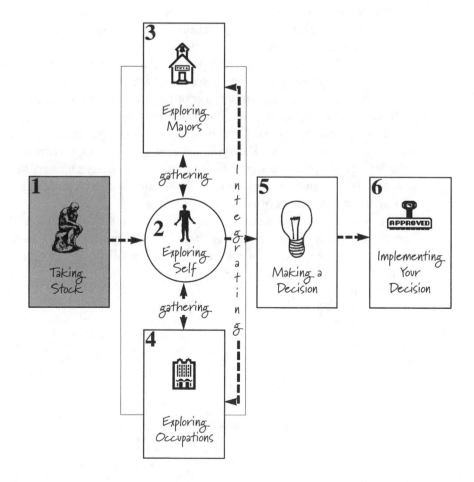

Two roads diverged in a wood, and I—
I took the one less traveled by,
And that has made all the difference.
From "The Road Not Taken" by Robert Frost

MAKING MAJOR AND CAREER DECISIONS

Whenever you are faced with two or more choices, you consciously or unconsciously use a process that usually leads to a decision. Because making decisions is such an integral part of daily life, learning to become an effective decision maker is important. Effective decision makers:

- experience more personal freedom because they take advantage of new opportunities that appear
- have greater control over their lives because they try to limit the influence of chance in determining their futures
- are more likely than indecisive persons to be satisfied with their decisions

Educational and career decisions are among the most important decisions you will make, because these choices largely determine how you will spend your future waking hours. Some students entering college may have decided which occupation to enter after graduation but may not be sure which college major will best lead them to that goal. Other students may be undecided about a future occupational area and yet easily select an academic major. Still others are totally undecided about a major and an occupational choice; they have made a decision to be "undecided" about both.

Of those who declare a major upon entering college, some will later have doubts about their earlier decisions. There are many reasons for wanting to change majors: a lack of interest in the coursework, discouragement over poor academic performance, or inability to meet the criteria established for that major.

To help you begin the process of selecting a college major and/or career field, this unit asks you to take stock of your current status. This involves both determining where you are in the decision-making process and analyzing why you are where you are. In this way, taking stock lays the foundation for understanding how you personally will approach this critical endeavor.

As you complete the stocktaking activities in this unit, you will find some that are divided into two sections, "A" and "B." If you are undecided, that is, totally uncertain of your choice of major and/or occupation, answer the set of questions marked "A"; if you are considering a change of major, answer the set of questions marked "B."

ACTIVITY: YOUR CURRENT MAJOR STATUS

Complete "A" if you are undecided; complete "B" if you are considering a change in major.

A. I am undecided about a major. (Check all that apply.)

❏ I don't have enough information about various majors.

❏ I don't have enough information about possible career fields to which majors may lead.

❏ I'm not sure about my ability to succeed in the coursework for certain majors.

❏ I have so many interests that I can't narrow my options.

❏ I don't have strong interests in anything, so I'm not sure which areas to explore.

❏ I'm not sure of my values, so I don't know what is important to me in a major or career area.

❏ I'm afraid to choose a major because it might be the wrong decision.

❏ I'm not sure what jobs will be available to me if I graduate with a certain major.

❏ I have difficulty making decisions in general.

❏ Other people have suggested majors, but I'm not sure they are right for me.

❏ Other reasons (be specific): _____
_____
_____
_____

Examine the reasons you checked. In what areas do they indicate you need help (for example, self, academic or occupational information, decision making)? Why?

_____

_____

OR

B. I am considering a change in major. (Check all that apply.)

❏ I didn't have enough information about this major when I chose it and have since found out it is not for me.

❏ I didn't want to enter college undecided about a major, so I signed up for one that seemed interesting at the time.

❏ I chose this major because other people strongly encouraged me in that direction.

❏ I discovered that the occupations related to this major do not appeal to me.

❏ I don't have strong enough abilities to succeed in the required coursework for this major.

❏ I'm not interested in the coursework required for this major.

❏ I'm not sure the values associated with this major (e.g., economic security) are as important to me now.

❏ I don't qualify for this program based on the major's entrance requirements.

❏ Other reasons (be specific): _____
_____
_____
_____

Examine the reasons you checked. What influenced you to choose your last major? Are any of these strong reasons for you to explore other majors? Why?

_____

_____

_____

ACTIVITY: YOUR CURRENT CAREER STATUS

Complete "A" if you are undecided; complete "B" if you are considering a change in major.

A. I am undecided about an occupational field. (Check all that apply.)

❏ I don't have enough information about various occupations.

❏ I don't have enough information about the relationships between occupations and academic majors.

❏ I'm not sure of the abilities needed in certain occupations.

❏ I have so many interests that I can't narrow my options.

❏ I don't have strong interests in anything, so I'm not sure which areas to explore.

❏ I'm not sure of my values, so I don't know what is important to me in selecting an occupational field.

❏ I'm afraid to choose an occupation because it might be the wrong decision.

❏ I'm not sure what specific jobs will be available to me as a result of the occupations I am considering.

❏ I have difficulty making decisions in general.

❏ Other people have suggested certain occupations, but I'm not sure they are right for me.

❏ Other reasons (be specific): _____

_____

_____

_____

Examine the reasons you checked. In what areas do they indicate you need help (for example, self, academic or occupational information, decision making)? Why?

_____

_____

_____

OR

B. I am considering a change in occupation. (Check all that apply.)

❏ I didn't have enough information about this occupation when I chose it and have since found out it is not for me

❏ I didn't want to enter college undecided about a major, so I selected an occupational area that seemed interesting at the time.

❏ I chose this occupation because other people strongly encouraged me in that direction.

❏ I discovered that the academic majors related to this occupation do not appeal to me.

❏ I don't have strong enough abilities to succeed in performing the work tasks in this occupation.

❏ I'm not interested in the work tasks involved in this occupation.

❏ I'm not sure the values associated with this occupation (e.g., economic security) are as important to me now.

❏ I don't qualify for entrance into the major required for this occupation.

❏ Other reasons (be specific): _____

_____

_____

_____

Examine the reasons you checked. What influenced you to choose your last occupation? Are any of these strong reasons for you to explore other occupational fields? Why?

_____

_____

_____

THE DECISION-MAKING PROCESS
Your Feelings About Decision Making

Whether you are undecided or considering a change in major, how you feel about making decisions in general plays an integral role in how you approach the process. Sometimes we ignore our feelings even though they may exert a strong influence on our decisions, consciously or unconsciously.

ACTIVITY: DISCOVERING YOUR FEELINGS

How do you feel now about choosing or changing your major? Place a check next to the adjectives that best describe your feelings:

❏ anxious	❏ disappointed	❏ frustrated	❏ pressured
❏ confused	❏ excited	❏ happy	❏ relaxed
❏ dejected	❏ fearful	❏ numb	❏ stressed

How do these feelings affect your motivation for engaging in the activities required to choose or change your major (for example, When I feel stressed, it's difficult for me to feel motivated)?

_____

_____

_____

If you are not motivated at this time, what do you think you could do to become motivated?

_____

_____

_____

Your Decision-Making Strategy

Theorists in the field of decision making identify different strategies people use when they are faced with both daily choices and more important but infrequent life decisions. The following activity lists strategies that several theorists have identified.

ACTIVITY: FINDING YOUR STRATEGY

Which of these decision-making strategies most closely resembles how you are approaching the decision of selecting or changing a major?

❑ **Procrastinator**—I know I must make a decision but will put it off as long as possible.

❑ **Impulsive**—I take the first choice that seems reasonable without looking at other majors or collecting information.

❑ **Fatalistic**—I will leave the decision to fate since I have very little control over it.

❑ **Agonizing**—I have invested so much time and thought into possible majors that I feel overwhelmed and can't decide.

❑ **Compliant**—I think it is best if someone else who knows more about the subject (e.g., parent, teacher, adviser) makes the decision for me.

❑ **Intuitive**—I will make a decision when it feels right.

❑ **Planful**—I will make a decision based on an orderly, rational process that requires solid information and reflection and involves both thinking and feeling.

How does the strategy you checked affect the way you did or will choose a major?

_____

_____

_____

If you checked a strategy other than "planful," what can you do to overcome any negative aspects of your approach?

_____

_____

_____

Your Decision-Making Style

Have you ever analyzed how you approach decisions? Over the years you have developed a personal decision-making style or set of behaviors that you use when confronted by a decision situation. Some styles are effective, while others may be counterproductive. You may use one style in major decision situations (e.g., choosing a major, buying a car) and a different style for smaller ones (e.g., what to wear, what to buy in the grocery store).

Decision theorist William Coscarelli determined that how you gather information and how you analyze it after you have collected it are important determinants of your decision-making style. You *gather* information either spontaneously or systematically; you *analyze* it either internally or externally. When these two dimensions are joined, four distinct decision-making styles emerge: spontaneous external, spontaneous internal, systematic external, and systematic internal.

- Spontaneous—You make a decision quickly, because it feels right; you know you can change it easily.
- Systematic—You collect all the necessary information first and then methodically weigh all the pros and cons before deciding.
- External—You talk with many people whose judgment you trust.
- Internal—You think about the situation and come to a decision on your own.

Activity: Understanding Your Style

Now apply these dimensions to your decision making to discover why you are undecided or why you decided to change your major or occupation. *Complete "A" if you are undecided; complete "B" if you are considering a change in major.*

A. My decision to be undecided about a major and/or occupation was

Spontaneous   **OR**   **Systematic**

- I changed my mind so many times, I couldn't decide.
- It just felt right not to make a decision.
- I know that once I decide, I may change my mind, so it's not that important.

- I collected a great deal of information from many sources, but still wasn't sure.
- I analyzed my skills and abilities to see how they matched certain majors, but I still wasn't sure.
- Once I make up my mind, I seldom change it, so I want to be sure before I make the decision.

External   **OR**   **Internal**

- I talked to my parents and friends about what to do.
- I consulted with my teachers and counselors.
- I considered the advice of others when choosing to remain undecided.

- I thought a lot about my situation before choosing to be undecided.
- I really didn't seek the advice of too many people.
- I examined all the information by myself but still couldn't decide.

Circle the style you think you used in choosing to be undecided:

spontaneous external   spontaneous internal   systematic external   systematic internal

B. My decision to change my major and/or occupation was

Spontaneous   **OR**   **Systematic**

- My other major/occupation just didn't feel right.
- I lost interest quickly in my last choice and started to think about changing.
- If my next decision doesn't work out, I can always choose another.

- I examined my situation carefully and decided to change.
- I gathered a great deal of information about my situation before deciding to change.
- I know it will take careful study and thought before I can make a new decision

External	**OR**	**Internal**

External

- I talked to many people about my situation before deciding to change.
- I weighed the advice of others who knew my situation and decided to change.
- My friends encouraged me to change.

OR   Internal

- I am changing only after a great deal of thought.
- I thought about my situation for some time before consulting with others.
- I am still reflecting on my decision to change and will continue to do so.

Circle the style you think you used in deciding to change your major or occupation:

    spontaneous external   spontaneous internal   systematic external   systematic internal

What do your answers suggest about how you tend to gather and analyze information before making a decision?

_____

_____

_____

Which style do you consider most effective in making realistic major and occupational decisions? Why?

_____

_____

_____

Your Gender and Decision Making

Prevailing gender-role stereotypes in American society influence the decision-making processes of both females and males in choosing a major and a career. During their childhood and adolescent years, American females hear messages from significant people in their lives, such as parents, grandparents, teachers, and coaches, that tend to limit their occupational choices. *Choose a career that will be compatible with marriage and a family* is frequently heard advice. Other messages encourage females to pass over or ignore opportunities in the trades (construction, carpentry, automotive mechanics) and in math- and science-related occupations (engineering, physics) because these occupational areas have traditionally been male-dominated and thus considered inappropriate for females. Additionally, many females are discouraged from taking advanced math and science courses in high school—courses necessary to pursue a college major in math and science fields and for succeeding in math- and science-oriented occupations. Given the subtle and frequently not-so-subtle messages sent to females, it is no wonder that they often choose from a limited number of occupations—the "helping" professions—teaching, social work, and nursing. Females who choose not to go to college often find themselves limited to secretarial or service-oriented jobs that, along with the helping professions, tend to be lower-paid positions.

The stereotypical messages often sent to American males are that they can do anything they want to do if they work hard enough. For example, the media—television, radio, and magazines—portray males in many different roles, promoting the notion that males have many careers from which to choose. On the other hand, like females, these stereotypical messages tend to limit their occupational choices. Males are told that they must pursue a career that enables them to be the main breadwinner of a family, and occupations such as child care, elementary teaching, and nursing are often portrayed as inappropriate for males. Somehow a male's masculinity, as well as his good sense, is questioned if he expresses an interest in these nurturing and female-dominated helping professions. The result of these stereotypes is that males are represented in a wide range of occupations and make substantially higher earnings than females, often with the same amount of education. Nevertheless, like females, the stereotypes have greatly affected males' choices of major and occupation for life, and many of them may not be pursuing their true interests.

We all have received stereotypical messages of some kind during our formative years. Perhaps you are not pursuing the occupation in which you are really interested. Perhaps the messages you have received have resulted in your limiting your own horizons.

ACTIVITY: REVEALING GENDER-ROLE STEREOTYPES

Take a few minutes and list some of the messages you think you received about appropriate roles and occupations for females and males while growing up.

_____

_____

_____

_____

_____

Do you think you have allowed these messages to limit your choices, or have you made choices with which you are satisfied?

_____

_____

_____

_____

If your choices have been limited, plan to rethink your occupational options as you complete the activities in this text.

Your Goals and Decision Making

Setting short- and long-term goals is an important part of decision making. Without goals you cannot estimate how your current choices will influence your future. In Unit Two you will examine your work values. Goals are simply values projected into the future, so identifying what is important to you will shape the major and career decisions you make now and in the future. Later, in Unit Six, you will be revisiting these goals.

ACTIVITY: SETTING YOUR GOALS

Think about the day after graduation and write down three goals you would like to accomplish by then.

Personal goal   (e.g., I will be a well-rounded, educated person.)

_____

_____

Academic goal   (e.g., I will graduate with at least a 3.0 grade point average.)

_____

_____

Career goal   (e.g., I will develop the skills and knowledge to be successful in the workplace.)

_____

_____

SUMMARY

As you read Unit One and worked through the activities, you took stock of your current situation and learned how your personal decision-making style has affected it and will affect it in the future. The stocktaking you did in this unit has prepared you for the next step in exploring possible academic and career directions. As indicated earlier, the decision-making process that you will be engaged in as you progress through this book is evolutionary, not static. You will gather information, identify alternatives, weigh them against your strengths and limitations, and ultimately decide on a direction to explore. You are in control of every aspect of this process.

ACTIVITY: SUMMARY

Check the appropriate column below to indicate how much you were aware of these elements in making previous decisions.

ELEMENTS OF DECISION MAKING	VERY MUCH AWARE	SOMEWHAT AWARE	NOT AWARE
1. understanding how I made past academic decisions			
2. understanding how I made past occupational decisions			
3. understanding my reasons for being undecided			
4. examining my feelings about making choices			
5. understanding the decision strategies I use			
6. examining my decision-making style			
7. examining gender-role stereotyping in regard to myself and my occupational choices			
8. need for compromise when choosing between equally desirable alternatives			
9. importance of setting personal, academic, and career goals			

If you were somewhat aware of or not aware of some of these elements, be sure to emphasize these as you begin the process of academic and career planning.

CASE STUDY: ASHLEY
(for undecided students)

Ashley entered college with her major listed as undecided. She had so many ideas about a college major that she could not decide on one. She thought she could choose a major during her first year after taking a few courses. She was concerned that some of the majors she was considering, such as English and history, might not lead to a specific job. At one time in high school, Ashley had decided to be a teacher since her mother was a teacher. Although she still felt this was a good profession for her, since she would have the same hours as her children some day, she had never felt fully committed to the idea.

As a sophomore, Ashley finds herself no closer to a choice of major than the day she entered college and is feeling rather depressed and frustrated. She realizes she needs to take stock of her situation and take some action toward making a decision soon.

Certain ideas and people have influenced Ashley's occupational decisions in the past. What or who have influenced yours?

_____

_____

_____

Why is she undecided? Why are you?

_____

_____

_____

What are her feelings at this point? What are yours?

_____

_____

_____

Ashley's views of herself and/or occupations might be influenced by gender-role stereotypes. Could yours be too? How?

_____

_____

_____

To begin the process of deciding on a major, what could Ashley do next? What next steps do you need to take?

_____

_____

_____

CASE STUDY: MANUEL

(for students changing majors)

Manuel is a sophomore business major and is making average grades in his business courses. He chose business because he felt it would lead him to a well-paying job. Manuel finds, however, that he has no interest in his business courses and keeps putting off scheduling courses that he should be taking. He has become very involved in the theater activities on his campus by volunteering as a stage manager. He is also considering auditioning for a role in the next student production. Manuel is very excited about his involvement with the theater department and is seriously considering changing to a theater major. When he mentions this to his family, they are very discouraging. He knows he needs to take stock of his situation in order to decide whether to change majors.

What has influenced Manuel's ideas about occupational choices in the past? What has influenced yours the most?

_____

_____

_____

What are Manuel's feelings about his current major? About changing majors? What are yours?

_____

_____

_____

What compromises might Manuel need to make if he chooses a theater major over a business major? What compromises might you need to make?

_____

_____

_____

What can Manuel do to help himself decide? What can you do?

_____

_____

_____

PERSONAL LOG #1

A personal log gives you a chance to record and reflect upon thoughts, insights, and feelings about yourself and the steps you are taking toward making academic and occupational decisions. Following is an example of how one person's log might begin.

Sample Log

I never really thought about how I make decisions. I didn't realize how much I depend on the opinions of others when faced with a decision. I'm always afraid of making the wrong decision and think others know better than I do.

Also, I have never really tested myself. I don't know what I am capable of doing. I like math but I have never been motivated to spend the time and effort to do as well as I think I can. I feel that I accept second-best from myself. I am going to start demanding more of myself.

Write down any thoughts or feelings about your situation that taking stock in this unit may have prompted.

_____

_____

_____

_____

_____

_____

_____

_____

_____

_____

_____

_____

_____

_____

UNIT TWO
Exploring Self

I should not talk so much about myself if
there were anybody else I know so well.

Thoreau

YOU ARE A UNIQUE PERSON, a unique blend of personality, interests, abilities, and values. This unit will help you explore your personal characteristics with a view toward understanding your vocational self-concept. Self-exploration is a critical step in making realistic academic and career decisions. A major and a career are among the most momentous decisions you will make in your life, and the better you understand what you value in a work environment, the better you will be able to choose.

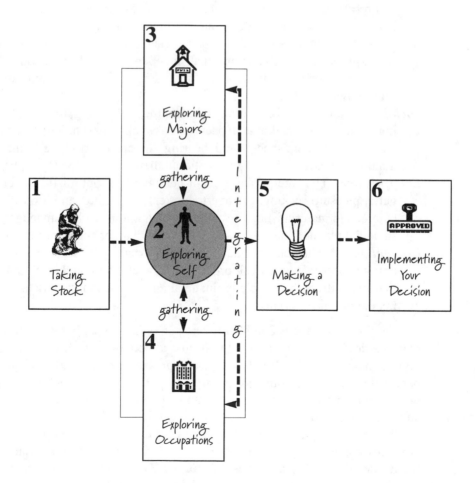

THE INFLUENCE OF PERSONALITY

Have you ever thought about how your personality might influence your educational and occupational choices? One career theorist, John Holland, has studied this idea in depth and suggests that your personality is reflected in the type of occupational environments or workplaces you choose. Holland suggests that your personality is a product of both your heredity and experiences and that these in turn influence your preferences for a variety of activities and tasks. Your preferences develop into leisure and school interests (and later work-related interests) from which you gain pleasure and satisfaction. As you engage in activities that are of great interest, you develop skills that later influence your educational and career choices.

After many years of research, Holland categorized workers into six personality types. He also divided all occupations into six work environments (using the same names) in which these types of workers might be satisfied. He theorizes that people will seek work environments that are compatible with their personalities. The six types and their descriptions follow:

Realistic.   People with a realistic type of personality are conforming, frank, materialistic, persistent, modest, practical, shy, and hardheaded. A few examples of occupations that might interest realistic types are mechanic, aircraft controller, computer operator, farmer, aviator, or electrical engineer.

Investigative.   Investigative personality types are described as analytical, independent, intellectual, pessimistic, introverted, critical, precise, methodical, curious, and reserved. They prefer occupations such as biologist, data analyst, veterinarian, medical technologist, computer engineer, or physician.

Artistic.   The artistic personality type is described as imaginative, creative, idealistic, expressive, intuitive, emotional, independent, and impractical. They tend to like occupations such as musician, actor, English teacher, interior designer, historian, writer, or artist.

Social.   Social people like activities that include informing, training, helping, or curing others. They are drawn to occupations such as psychologist, social worker, elementary teacher, speech and hearing therapist, coach, criminologist, nurse, athletic director, clergy, or occupational therapist.

Enterprising.   The enterprising type of personality is optimistic, adventurous, energetic, pleasure seeking, extroverted, attention getting, ambitious, impulsive, sociable, and materialistic. They prefer occupations such as manager, salesperson, financial planner, business executive, politician, or sports promoter.

Conventional.   The conventional personality type is persistent, conforming, conscientious, obedient, practical, orderly, thrifty, efficient, and inhibited. Occupations that may attract them include financial analyst, accountant, data analyst, banker, tax expert, or librarian.

Obviously no one is completely one personality type, but a combination. As you read the descriptions, you probably found adjectives in each type that describe you. Although attributes of all six types may be present, Holland indicates that two to three personality types are dominant in any one person. Thus matching your personality with compatible work environments can help you narrow down the general academic and occupational areas you will want to explore.

The activities in this unit draw upon Holland's ideas about personality types and how they connect with work environments. A set of categories similar to Holland's is the framework for the activities that follow. These activities will help you organize your interests, aptitudes and abilities, work environments, and work values into categories or patterns that can help you narrow down your options. The categories are Engineering/Technical *(Realistic)*, Arts/Humanities *(Artistic)*, Science *(Investigative)*, Human Services/Social Sciences *(Social)*, Business/People-Oriented *(Enterprising)*, and Business/Data-Oriented *(Conventional)*.

After completing the activities in this unit, you will be able to develop a personal profile that incorporates your many personal attributes. You will use this profile in the educational and occupational exploration activities in the following units. Note: If you wish to pursue Holland's ideas further, use the Web site www.self-directed-search.com or obtain a copy of *Making Vocational Choices: A Theory of Vocational Personalities and Work Environment* by John L. Holland (1997).

ACTIVITY: FINDING YOUR INTERESTS

An interest is a preference for certain types of activities. Identifying your interests is an important part of academic and career decision making because, as mentioned earlier, you are more likely to be satisfied with your occupation if it is compatible with your interests. This activity is only a brief summary of what you might find interesting in the six general career areas. (In Unit Three you will determine your interest in academic majors in these same areas.)

Check the box for each activity that interests you:

Engineering/Technical
❑ Fix electrical appliances or equipment
❑ Study the physical sciences
❑ Build houses
❑ Design computer hardware
❑ Build or operate radio or television equipment
❑ Develop software programs
❑ Work on cars
❑ Work to preserve the environment
❑ Work with animals
❑ Solve mechanical problems
❑ Design landscape areas

Arts/Humanities
❑ Play in an orchestra or band
❑ Decorate your room
❑ Take art classes
❑ Write poetry or short stories
❑ Act in theatrical productions
❑ Take photographs
❑ Work on a newspaper
❑ Sculpt wood or clay
❑ Take modern dance or ballet
❑ Direct radio or television
❑ Study history
❑ Learn languages

Science
❑ Study the human body
❑ Do science experiments
❑ Design buildings
❑ Operate laboratory apparatus
❑ Study the oceans
❑ Program computers
❑ Solve mathematical problems
❑ Play chess
❑ Study animal behavior

Business/People-Oriented
❑ Sell products in a store
❑ Manage your own business
❑ Help others find employment
❑ Be involved in class elections
❑ Be the boss in business or industry
❑ Direct or manage a group of salespeople
❑ Persuade people to do it your way
❑ Be on a debate team
❑ Set up a law practice

Human Services/Social Sciences

- ❑ Work with people in parks or recreation
- ❑ Teach elementary school children
- ❑ Help people with personal problems
- ❑ Help people who are ill
- ❑ Work with people in religious settings
- ❑ Help people develop their physical abilities
- ❑ Work with people who have disabilities
- ❑ Supervise workers in a business
- ❑ Be a good friend
- ❑ Volunteer in a hospital
- ❑ Study psychology

Business/Data-Oriented

- ❑ Learn to keyboard
- ❑ Work as a bank teller
- ❑ Design Web sites
- ❑ Take a course in statistics
- ❑ Develop an accounting system for a business
- ❑ Assist others in managing their finances
- ❑ Teach business education
- ❑ Do general office work
- ❑ Supervise a quality control project
- ❑ Be a financial analyst

PROFILE 1: YOUR INTERESTS

List the three career areas that *best* represent your interests:

_____

_____

List the one career area that *least* represents your interests:

_____

_____

ACTIVITY: UNDERSTANDING YOUR APTITUDES AND ABILITIES

Abilities generally are regarded as talents or skills you already possess, while *aptitudes* are thought of as areas in which you have potential to develop your talents or skills. The U.S. Department of Labor identifies several work task areas and provides definitions of aptitudes and abilities necessary to achieve in each area.

As you read the work task definitions that follow, consider your own level of achievement or potential for achievement in each work task area, comparing yourself to your peers.

Mechanical reasoning (things):

understanding how different kinds of mechanical things work

Space relations (things):

looking at flat drawings or pictures of objects and forming mental images of them in three dimensions (height, width, depth); picturing how objects would look if seen from different angles

Language skills (people):

using the English language correctly in order to communicate and present ideas clearly; being able to identify incorrect use of the English language

Numerical skills (data):

performing basic math operations (e.g., addition, subtraction, multiplication)

Reading comprehension (ideas):

reading and understanding different types of material

Manual dexterity (things):

moving the hands with ease and skill; working with the hands in placing and turning motions

Leadership skills (people):

coordinating, supervising, or directing others, projects, or activities

Clerical skills (data):

ability to follow directions and perform detailed clerical tasks quickly and accurately

Artistic ability (ideas):

designing or producing an art form (e.g., music, sculpture, dance)

Creative skills (ideas):

inventing, designing, or developing new ideas

Rate yourself on the following table (p. 20), circling the number that best represents your level of ability or potential ability in each area.

Work Task Area

Rating	Mechanical Reasoning (Things)	Numerical Skills (Data)	Space Relations (Things)	Reading Comprehension (Ideas)	Language Skills (People)
High	7	7	7	7	7
	6	6	6	6	6
	5	5	5	5	5
Average	4	4	4	4	4
	3	3	3	3	3
	2	2	2	2	2
Low	1	1	1	1	1

Rating	Manual Dexterity (Things)	Leadership Skills (People)	Artistic Ability (Ideas)	Clerical Skills (Data)	Creative Skills (Ideas)
High	7	7	7	7	7
	6	6	6	6	6
	5	5	5	5	5
Average	4	4	4	4	4
	3	3	3	3	3
	2	2	2	2	2
Low	1	1	1	1	1

Each work task area is related to working primarily with people, things, data, or ideas, which are, in turn, correlated with the career areas already outlined:

People
  • Human Services/Social Sciences
  • Business/People-Oriented

Data
  • Science
  • Business/Data-Oriented

Things
  • Arts/Humanities
  • Science
  • Engineering/Technical

Ideas
  • Science
  • Arts/Humanities

PROFILE 2: YOUR APTITUDES AND POTENTIAL ABILITIES

Reviewing the previous activity, count the number of times you circled 5, 6, or 7 (high) in each work task area.

People	**Things**	**Data**	**Ideas**
_____	_____	_____	_____

Based on your scores for these four task areas and the career areas associated with them, determine which two or three career areas describe you best:

_____   _____   _____

ACTIVITY: ESTABLISHING YOUR PREFERRED WORK ENVIRONMENT

People differ in their choice of work environments. For example, some are impatient with long, slow jobs, while others do not mind working on one project for a long time. Others like to lead at work, while some much prefer to follow the lead of someone else. Preferences in various work situations are to some extent determined by personality traits. Taking time to assess your preferred style of interacting in work situations can assist you with academic and career planning now. The more you know about yourself, the greater your likelihood of making satisfactory educational and career decisions.

Check each phrase that describes a work situation you prefer.

Engineering/Technical

- ❏ Like to perform activities requiring motor coordination skills and physical strength
- ❏ Like action solutions rather than tasks involving verbal or interpersonal skills
- ❏ Like activities that are scientific or mechanical rather than cultural or esthetic
- ❏ Like to work with tools or machines
- ❏ Like to take a concrete approach to problem solving rather than an abstract or theoretical one
- ❏ Like to work with animals

Human Services/Social Sciences

- ❏ Like teaching or helping situations
- ❏ Like situations with close interpersonal relationships
- ❏ Like to solve problems by discussing them with others
- ❏ Like practical tasks
- ❏ Like situations where communication with others is important
- ❏ Like situations where individuals are recognized for their contributions

Arts/Humanities

- ❏ Like situations where self-expression is valued
- ❏ Like to work alone
- ❏ Like tasks involving physical skills
- ❏ Dislike structure in the work setting
- ❏ Like cultural and esthetic activities
- ❏ Like to be creative

Business/People-Oriented

- ❏ Like tasks that are adventurous
- ❏ Willing to exert a lot of energy at work
- ❏ Like to direct and persuade others
- ❏ Like to use communications skills
- ❏ Like to be a leader in the work setting
- ❏ Like practical tasks rather than theoretical ones

Science

- ❏ Like to manipulate ideas, work, and symbols rather than exhibit physical or social skills
- ❏ Like originality and creativity
- ❏ Like theoretical problems or tasks
- ❏ Like to work independently and not particularly people oriented
- ❏ Like to understand the ideas behind the work
- ❏ Like to think rather than act or organize

Business/Data-Oriented

- ❏ Like structured work settings with precise work
- ❏ Don't mind following rules and regulations
- ❏ Dislike work requiring physical strength
- ❏ Like situations emphasizing order and harmony
- ❏ Like definite standards of right and wrong
- ❏ Like others to make the major decisions

PROFILE 3: YOUR PREFERRED WORK ENVIRONMENT

Review the phrases you checked. Most people enjoy a combination of these six work situations but, if forced to choose, which three work situations seem to suit you best?

_____   _____   _____

ACTIVITY: ASSESSING YOUR WORK VALUES

Although you may experience the same values in many career areas, certain areas emphasize some values more explicitly than others. Read through this list, thinking about your future work. Then choose the four values most important to you and rank them, with "l" being the most important.

_____ Achievement—work that gives me a feeling of accomplishment

_____ Security—work that provides me with the certainty of having a job even in hard times

_____ Creativity—work that permits me to invent new things, design new products, or develop new ideas

_____ Management—work that permits me to plan and lay out work for others to do

_____ Surroundings—work that is carried out under pleasant conditions: not too hot, cold, noisy, dirty, etc.

_____ Supervisory relations—work that is carried out under a supervisor who is fair and with whom I can get along

_____ Way of life—work that permits me to live the kind of life I choose and to be the type of person I want to be

_____ Associates—work that brings me into contact with fellow workers whom I like

_____ Esthetics—work that permits me to make beautiful things and to contribute beauty to the world

_____ Prestige—work that gives me standing in the eyes of others and evokes respect

_____ Independence—work that permits me to work in my own way, as fast or as slow as I wish

_____ Variety—work that provides me with an opportunity to do different types of jobs

_____ Economic returns—work that pays well and enables me to have the things I want

_____ Altruism—work that enables me to contribute to the welfare of others

_____ Intellectual stimulation—work that provides me with opportunity for independent thinking and for learning how and why things work

The following work values are associated with the different career areas. Review your top four choices and transfer them to the following list to determine which career areas most closely reflect your current work values.

Engineering/Technology

- ❏ Achievement
- ❏ Security
- ❏ Economic returns
- ❏ Independence

Human Services/Social Sciences

- ❏ Management
- ❏ Supervisory relations
- ❏ Associates
- ❏ Altruism
- ❏ Prestige

Arts/Humanities

- ❏ Independence
- ❏ Variety
- ❏ Intellectual stimulation
- ❏ Esthetics
- ❏ Way of life
- ❏ Creativity

Business/People-Oriented

- ❏ Management
- ❏ Achievement
- ❏ Associates
- ❏ Economic returns
- ❏ Variety

Science

- ❏ Independence
- ❏ Variety
- ❏ Prestige
- ❏ Creativity
- ❏ Way of life
- ❏ Intellectual stimulation

Business/Data-Oriented

- ❏ Supervisory relations
- ❏ Security
- ❏ Surroundings
- ❏ Achievement

PROFILE 4: YOUR WORK VALUES

Which two or three career areas seem to reflect your work values most?

_____   _____   _____

ACTIVITY: SUMMARIZING YOUR FOUR PROFILES

To summarize what you have learned about yourself in this unit, complete the following profile summary. Review each of your four profiles and circle the career areas that best describe you in each of the areas.

INTERESTS	Engineering/Technology Human Services/ Social Sciences	Science Business/People- Oriented	Arts/Humanities Business/ Data-Oriented
APTITUDES AND POTENTIAL ABILITIES	Engineering/Technology Human Services/ Social Sciences	Science Business/People- Oriented	Arts/Humanities Business/ Data-Oriented
WORK ENVIRONMENT	Engineering/Technology Human Services/ Social Sciences	Science Business/People- Oriented	Arts/Humanities Business/Data- Oriented
WORK VALUES	Engineering/Technology Human Services/ Social Sciences	Science Business/People- Oriented	Arts/Humanities Business/Data- Oriented

PROFILE 5: YOUR OVERALL CAREER AREAS

When you consider the previous four profiles completed in this unit, which three of the six career areas seem to fit you best overall? (You will use this information later to complete activities in Unit Four.)

_____   _____   _____

SUMMARY

Throughout this unit you have been involved in assessing your strengths—the personal characteristics that make you a unique person. In the next unit you will relate this information to possible academic majors, so now is the time to think about what you have learned about yourself.

What are your most outstanding strengths?

_____

_____

_____

What limitations have you identified?

_____

_____

_____

How does this information about yourself fit with your past or current ideas about academic majors and career areas in which you may be interested?

_____

_____

_____

INTERNET RESOURCES FOR SELF-ASSESSMENT

Career Assessments.   You might want to use other career inventories to measure your interests, abilities or skills, personality characteristics, or work values. You can take the following inventories or surveys on the Internet:

- _The Strong Interest Inventory_ is administered from the publisher's Web site at http://www.cpp-db.com/ products/strong.
- _The Self-Directed Search_ is administered from the publisher's Web site at http://www.self-directed-search.com.
- _Campbell Interest and Skill Survey_ is administered from http://www.profiler.com/ciss.
- _The Keirsey Character Sorter,_ a personality-like inventory, can be taken at http://www.keirsey.com.
- _SkillScan_ is administered from http:www.skillscan.net.

Career Information.   The Internet has many of the most current sources of occupational information. The following Web sites specialize in databases and searches and include information about occupations, colleges, academic majors, scholarships, and financial aid:

- O^*Net (which has replaced the U.S. Department of Labor's _Dictionary of Occupational Titles_) is a database that describes more than 1000 occupations in detail. It can be found at http://www.doleta.gov/ programs/onet.
- The _Occupational Outlook Handbook (OOH),_ also published by the Department of Labor, and provides extensive information about 250 occupations at http://www.bls.gov/oco. The _Occupational Outlook Quarterly_ provides the latest information and projections on a variety of topics relating to the labor market at the same site.

The Department of Labor is engaged in ongoing development of four Web sites that together comprise _America's Career Kit._ They include _American's Learning Exchange_ at http://www.alx.org; _America's Job Bank_ and _America's Talent Bank,_ both at http://www.ajb.dni.us; and _CareerInfoNet_ at http://www.acinet.org. The sites include occupational information, labor market information, and a resource section that links to many other Web sites providing similar information.

CASE STUDY: SABRINA

Sabrina is undecided about a major. She is very interested in sports but is not sure how to pursue that area in a major or career field. While she has participated in sports throughout her life, she knows she does not have the aptitude to be a professional athlete. Using the *Occupational Outlook Handbook* online at www.bls.gov/oco, Sabrina confirms her interest in sports. She is now considering a career in coaching, sports writing, or sports business. She knows she has the ability to do all three.

What other information does Sabrina need at this point? What do *you* need?

Where can she obtain this information? Where can *you*?

To move along in the choice process, what could Sabrina do next? What could *you* do?

CASE STUDY: KEVIN

Kevin began college as a business major. Although he is doing well academically, he isn't sure business is what he wants. He feels there was something missing when he made his choice spontaneously during the freshman orientation program. He is bored with his math and economics courses and is beginning to feel uncomfortable about his initial choice. His adviser suggests he return to an important part of academic and career decision making: self-assessment. He discovers his highest interests and abilities are in the Arts/Humanities area. He finds his strongest values to be creativity and esthetics. Kevin took many art courses in high school and is an avid photographer. He wonders if he should change to a major that reflects his interest in art. He is concerned about the types of jobs he could get with such a major, however.

What next steps should Kevin take to determine if art-related majors would be better for him than his current business direction?

_____

_____

_____

_____

_____

What next steps should you take to explore your new ideas about majors?

_____

_____

PERSONAL LOG #2

Summarize what you have learned from this unit and class discussions. What patterns are visible? What insights do you have about your interests, strengths, and limitations? What values have you identified? How are you going to use this personal knowledge?

_____

_____

_____

_____

_____

_____

_____

_____

_____

_____

_____

_____

_____

_____

_____

_____

_____

_____

_____

_____

_____

UNIT THREE
Exploring Majors

Seek for truth in the groves of Academe.

Horace

UNDERSTANDING THE MAJORS that are available to you is the next important phase of deciding on your future academic direction. Gathering information from primary sources is an important part of the decision-making process. In this unit, you will begin exploring majors from a broad perspective in various two-year, four-year, and graduate programs. You will then narrow these possibilities down to two or three major alternatives that are available at your institution.

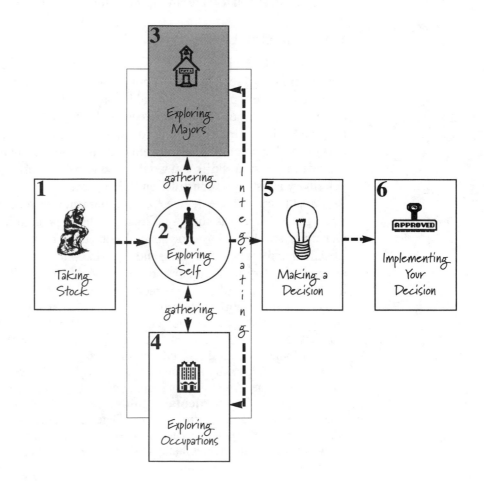

29

EXPLORING ACADEMIC MAJOR POSSIBILITIES

The first three activities in this unit provide three different avenues for identifying academic alternatives that you might want to explore. You will examine the following:

1. **Areas of study** identified by the *Higher Education General Information Survey* (HEGIS) system published by the National Institute of Education. Even though the number of majors on your campus will be small when compared with the list identified by this government survey of all higher education institutions, check through the complete list anyway. Interest patterns indicated by your choices might suggest general academic fields you will want to explore in more depth.
2. The **undergraduate majors** available at your institution. From your institution's catalogue or Web site, or from your instructor, obtain a list of majors offered at your college or university. By checking any and all that seem interesting, you can identify several that you will want to explore further.
3. **General areas of interest** in which majors are categorized. Sample majors are categorized by the interest areas identified in Unit Two. This activity offers another perspective for identifying possible fields of study.

At the end of these three activities, you will be asked to synthesize the majors on all three lists. Pay particular attention to those that emerge from two or more of the activities and that you feel are strong and realistic enough to warrant more detailed study.

Understanding Degree Programs

Before considering possible majors, you need to understand how majors on your campus are organized (by college, school, or department) and how undergraduate degrees are created. The type of educational institution that you attend will determine the requirements for an undergraduate technical, associate's, or baccalaureate degree. An associate's degree may fulfill the course requirements for the first two years of a baccalaureate degree or may be a terminal degree itself. A two-year technical degree can provide the specific skills you would need to begin working in an occupation such as veterinary assistant or construction technology.

Most baccalaureate degrees require that students meet academic requirements in three general areas, as shown in Figure 2 and explained in the next few paragraphs. Generally speaking, basic or general education requirements are taken during the freshman and sophomore years, and departmental or college and major requirements are concentrated in the junior and senior years. In some cases a specific course may meet both a basic and a college requirement.

General Education Requirements.   The first area of requirements includes general or basic education requirements such as natural sciences, social sciences, and humanities. Such courses are intended to broaden your intellectual base and provide a stronger foundation for the specific subject matter in your discipline. General or basic education requirements are the foundation for the baccalaureate educational structure. Obtain a list of general requirements from your college bulletin or your instructor.

College or Departmental Requirements.   The next level of requirements are generally viewed as departmental or college requirements. These usually involve more specific areas of knowledge, such as foreign language or mathematics. In Figure 2 this is shown as the middle layer. Obtain a list of departmental or college requirements from the department or your instructor.

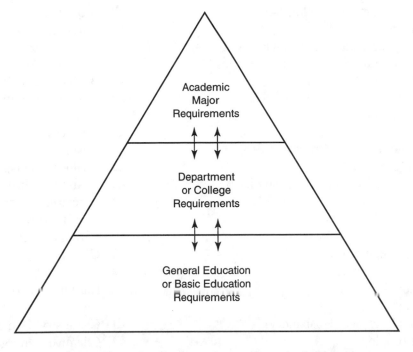

Figure 2   Example of a baccalaureate curricular structure.

Academic Major Requirements.   The final level of coursework is that required for the academic major itself. These courses provide in-depth knowledge pertaining to a specific discipline, such as history, architecture, business economics, or philosophy, or even more specialized areas within such disciplines. In Figure 2 these courses fit into the top portion of the triangle. Obtain a list of academic major requirements from the department or your instructor.

Minors and Electives.   Some degree programs allow a certain number of credit hours to be used in coursework in another academic department that is designated as a "minor." These courses are viewed as broadening your knowledge in a completely different area or in a field related to your major. Other credit hours may be designated as "electives." These are hours counted toward graduation that are not part of majors or minors. (Some majors may "suggest" or prescribe that certain coursework be used to fulfill these elective hours.) Using these credit hours wisely can expand the breadth of your knowledge and help you learn about areas that are of personal interest.

ACTIVITY: EXPLORING HEGIS AREAS OF STUDY

Check each area of study that holds or may hold some interest for you. If you do not know anything specific about the major, but the name conveys a positive feeling, go ahead and check it.

❏ Accounting
❏ Administration, Business
❏ Administration, Educational
❏ Administration, Hospital and Health Care
❏ Administration, Special Education
❏ Administration, Public

❏ Adult and Continuing Education
❏ Advertising
❏ Aerospace, Aeronautical, and Astronautical Engineering
❏ Aerospace Science (Air Force ROTC)
❏ African-American Studies (Culture)

❏ African Languages (Non-Semitic)
❏ African Studies
❏ Agricultural and Farm Management
❏ Agricultural and Forest Technologies
❏ Agricultural Business
❏ Agricultural Economics
❏ Agricultural Engineering
❏ Agriculture, General
❏ Agronomy (Field Crops and Crop Management)
❏ American Indian Cultural Studies
❏ American Studies
❏ Analytical Chemistry
❏ Anatomy
❏ Animal Pathology
❏ Animal Pharmacology
❏ Animal Physiology
❏ Animal Psychology
❏ Animal Science (Husbandry)
❏ Anthropology
❏ Applied Design
❏ Applied Mathematics
❏ Arabic
❏ Archeology
❏ Architectural Engineering
❏ Architecture
❏ Architecture, Landscape
❏ Architecture, Naval
❏ Architecture, Urban
❏ Art (Painting, Drawing, Sculpting)
❏ Art, Commercial
❏ Art Education
❏ Art History and Appreciation
❏ Asian Studies, General
❏ Astronomy
❏ Astrophysics
❏ Atmospheric Sciences and Meteorology
❏ Audiology
❏ Bacteriology
❏ Banking and Finance
❏ Biblical Languages
❏ Biochemistry
❏ Bioengineering and Biomedical Engineering
❏ Biology, Cell
❏ Biology, General
❏ Biology, Marine
❏ Biology, Molecular
❏ Biomedical Communication
❏ Biometrics and Biostatistics
❏ Biophysics

❏ Biostatistics
❏ Black Culture
❏ Botany, General
❏ Business, Agricultural
❏ Business and Commerce, General
❏ Business, Commerce, and Distributive Education
❏ Business Economics
❏ Business, International
❏ Business Management and Administration
❏ Business Statistics
❏ Cafeteria Management
❏ Cell Biology (Cytology, Cell Physiology)
❏ Ceramic Engineering
❏ Ceramics
❏ Chemical Engineering (including Petroleum Refining)
❏ Chemistry, Analytical
❏ Chemistry, General (except Biochemistry)
❏ Chemistry, Inorganic
❏ Chemistry, Organic
❏ Chemistry, Pharmaceutical
❏ Chemistry, Physical
❏ Child Development
❏ Chinese
❏ Chiropractic
❏ Cinematography
❏ City, Community, and Regional Planning
❏ Civil, Construction, and Transportation Engineering
❏ Classics
❏ Clinical Psychology
❏ Clinical Social Work
❏ Clothing and Textiles
❏ Commerce, Education
❏ Commercial Arts
❏ Communication, Biomedical
❏ Communication, Engineering
❏ Communications, General
❏ Communications Media (use of videotape, films, etc. oriented toward Radio/TV)
❏ Community College Education
❏ Community Planning
❏ Community Services, General
❏ Comparative Literature
❏ Computer and Information Sciences, General
❏ Computer Programming
❏ Conservation, Soil
❏ Construction Engineering
❏ Consumer Economics and Home Management

❏ Continuing Education
❏ Corrections
❏ Counseling
❏ Counseling, Psychology for
❏ Creative Writing
❏ Criminology
❏ Crop Management
❏ Culture, African American
❏ Culture, American Indian
❏ Culture, Mexican American
❏ Curriculum and Instruction
❏ Cytology
❏ Dairy Science (Husbandry)
❏ Dance
❏ Data Processing
❏ Debate
❏ Decoration, Home
❏ Demography
❏ Dental Hygiene
❏ Dental Specialties (beyond D.D.S. or D.M.D.)
❏ Dental Technologies
❏ Dentistry
❏ Design, Applied
❏ Design, Fashion
❏ Design, General Environmental
❏ Design, Interior
❏ Developmental Psychology
❏ Dietetics
❏ Distributive Education
❏ Dramatic Arts
❏ Drawing
❏ Driver Education
❏ Earth Science, General
❏ East Asian Studies
❏ Eastern European Studies
❏ Ecology
❏ Economics
❏ Economics, Agricultural
❏ Economics, Business
❏ Economics, Consumer
❏ Education, Adult and Continuing
❏ Educational Administration
❏ Educational Psychology
❏ Educational Statistics and Research
❏ Educational Supervision
❏ Educational Testing, Evaluation, and Measurement
❏ Education, Art
❏ Education, Business, Commerce, and Distribution

❏ Education, Driver
❏ Education, Elementary
❏ Education, General
❏ Education, Health
❏ Education, Higher
❏ Education, History and Philosophy of
❏ Education, Industrial Arts, Vocational, and Technical
❏ Education, Junior and Community College
❏ Education, Junior High School
❏ Education, Kindergarten
❏ Education, Mathematics
❏ Education of the Culturally Disadvantaged
❏ Education of the Deaf
❏ Education of the Emotionally Disturbed
❏ Education of the Gifted
❏ Education of the Mentally Impaired
❏ Education of the Multiply Impaired
❏ Education of the Physically Impaired
❏ Education of the Visually Impaired
❏ Education, Music
❏ Education, Physical
❏ Education, Reading
❏ Education, Religious
❏ Education, Remedial
❏ Education, Secondary
❏ Education, General Special
❏ Electrical, Electronic, and Communications Engineering
❏ Electronic Engineering
❏ Elementary Education, General
❏ Embryology
❏ Engineering, Aerospace, Aeronautical, and Astronomical
❏ Engineering, Agricultural
❏ Engineering, Architectural
❏ Engineering, Biomedical
❏ Engineering, Ceramic
❏ Engineering, Chemical
❏ Engineering, Civil, Construction, and Transportation
❏ Engineering, Electrical, Electronic, and Communications
❏ Engineering, Environmental and Sanitary
❏ Engineering, General
❏ Engineering, Geological
❏ Engineering, Geophysical
❏ Engineering, Industrial and Management
❏ Engineering, Marine
❏ Engineering, Materials

❏ Engineering, Mechanical
❏ Engineering, Mechanics
❏ Engineering, Metallurgical
❏ Engineering, Mining and Mineral
❏ Engineering, Nuclear
❏ Engineering, Ocean
❏ Engineering, Petroleum (except Refining)
❏ Engineering, Physics
❏ Engineering, Technologies
❏ Engineering, Textile
❏ English, General
❏ English Literature
❏ English, Teaching as a Foreign Language
❏ Entomology
❏ Environmental and Sanitary Engineering
❏ Environmental Design, General
❏ European Studies, General
❏ Experimental Psychology
❏ Family Life Education
❏ Family Relations and Child Development
❏ Farm Management
❏ Fashion Design
❏ Field Crops
❏ Finance
❏ Fine Arts, General
❏ Fish, Game, and Wildlife Management
❏ Floriculture
❏ Foods and Nutrition (including Dietetics)
❏ Food Science and Technology
❏ Foreign Languages
❏ Foreign Language, Teaching English as a
❏ Forensic Science
❏ Forestry
❏ French
❏ Fruit Production
❏ Game Management
❏ Geochemistry
❏ Geography
❏ Geological Engineering
❏ Geology
❏ Geophysical Engineering
❏ Geophysics and Seismology
❏ Genetics
❏ German
❏ Government
❏ Greek, Classical
❏ Guidance and Counseling
❏ Health Care Administration
❏ Health Education
❏ Health Professions, General

❏ Health, Public
❏ Hebrew
❏ Higher Education, General
❏ Histology
❏ History
❏ History of Education
❏ Home Decoration and Home Equipment
❏ Home Economics, General
❏ Home Management
❏ Horticulture (Fruit and Vegetable Production)
❏ Hospital and Health Care Administration
❏ Hotel and Restaurant Management
❏ Human Pathology
❏ Human Pharmacology
❏ Human Physiology
❏ Indian (Asiatic)
❏ Industrial and Management Engineering
❏ Industrial Arts, Vocational, and Technical Education
❏ Industrial Psychology
❏ Industrial Relations
❏ Information and Computer Sciences, General
❏ Information Sciences and Systems
❏ Inorganic Chemistry
❏ Institutional Management and Cafeteria Management
❏ Insurance
❏ Interior Decoration
❏ Interior Design
❏ International Business
❏ International Public Service (except Diplomatic)
❏ International Relations
❏ Investments and Securities
❏ Islamic Studies
❏ Italian
❏ Japanese
❏ Jewelry
❏ Journalism (Printed Media)
❏ Junior and Community College Education
❏ Junior High School Education
❏ Kindergarten Education
❏ Labor and Industrial Relations
❏ Landscape Architecture
❏ Languages, Biblical
❏ Languages, Foreign
❏ Latin
❏ Latin American Studies
❏ Law
❏ Law Enforcement and Corrections

❏ Library Science, General
❏ Linguistics
❏ Literature, Comparative
❏ Literature, English
❏ Management, Agricultural and Farm
❏ Management, Business
❏ Management, Cafeteria
❏ Management, Engineering
❏ Management, Fish, Game, and Wildlife
❏ Management, Home
❏ Management, Hotel and Restaurant
❏ Management, Institutional
❏ Management, Natural Resources
❏ Management, Parks and Recreation
❏ Management, Personnel
❏ Management, Range
❏ Management, Soils
❏ Marine Biology
❏ Marine Engineering
❏ Marketing and Purchasing
❏ Materials Engineering
❏ Mathematics, Applied
❏ Mathematics, Education
❏ Mathematics, General
❏ Mechanical Engineering
❏ Mechanics, Engineering
❏ Medical Laboratory Technologies
❏ Medical Record Librarianship
❏ Medicine (M.D.)
❏ Metallurgical Engineering
❏ Metallurgy
❏ Metalsmithing
❏ Meteorology
❏ Mexican American Culture Studies
❏ Microbiology
❏ Middle Eastern Studies
❏ Military Science (Army ROTC)
❏ Mining and Mineral Engineering
❏ Molecular Biology
❏ Molecular Physics
❏ Music (Liberal Arts)
❏ Music (Performing, Composition, Theory)
❏ Music Education
❏ Music History and Appreciation (Musicology)
❏ Music, Religious
❏ Natural Resources Management
❏ Naval Architecture and Marine Engineering
❏ Naval Science (Navy and Marines ROTC)
❏ Neuroscience
❏ Nuclear Engineering

❏ Nuclear Physics
❏ Nursery Science
❏ Nursing
❏ Nutrition
❏ Nutrition, Scientific (excluding Home Economics and Dietetics)
❏ Occupational Therapy
❏ Ocean Engineering
❏ Oceanography
❏ Operations Research
❏ Optometry
❏ Organic Chemistry
❏ Ornamental Horticulture (Floriculture, Nursery Science)
❏ Osteopathic Medicine (D.O.)
❏ Pacific Area Studies
❏ Painting
❏ Paleontology
❏ Parks and Recreation Management
❏ Pathology, Human and Animal
❏ Pathology, Plant
❏ Pathology, Speech
❏ Personnel Management
❏ Petroleum Engineering (except Refining)
❏ Pharmaceutical Chemistry
❏ Pharmacology, Human and Animal
❏ Pharmacology, Plant
❏ Pharmacy
❏ Philology
❏ Philosophy
❏ Philosophy of Education
❏ Phonetics
❏ Photography
❏ Physical Chemistry
❏ Physical Education
❏ Physical Sciences, General
❏ Physical Therapy
❏ Physics, Engineering
❏ Physics, General (except Biophysics)
❏ Physics, Molecular
❏ Physics, Nuclear
❏ Physiological Psychology
❏ Physiology, Cell
❏ Physiology, Human and Animal
❏ Physiology, Plant
❏ Planning, City, Community, and Regional
❏ Plant Pathology
❏ Plant Pharmacology
❏ Plant Physiology
❏ Podiatry (Pod.D. or D.P.)

- ❏ Political Science and Government
- ❏ Poultry Science
- ❏ Pre-Elementary Education (Kindergarten)
- ❏ Psychology, Clinical
- ❏ Psychology, Developmental
- ❏ Psychology, Educational
- ❏ Psychology, Experimental (Animal and Human)
- ❏ Psychology for Counseling
- ❏ Psychology, General
- ❏ Psychology, Industrial
- ❏ Psychology, Physiological
- ❏ Psychology, Social
- ❏ Psychology, Statistics in
- ❏ Psychometrics
- ❏ Public Address
- ❏ Public Administration
- ❏ Public Health
- ❏ Public Service, International (except Diplomatic)
- ❏ Public Utilities
- ❏ Purchasing
- ❏ Radiobiology
- ❏ Radiologic Technologies
- ❏ Radio/Television
- ❏ Range Management
- ❏ Reading Education
- ❏ Real Estate
- ❏ Recreation Management
- ❏ Regional Planning
- ❏ Religious Education
- ❏ Religious Music
- ❏ Religious Planning
- ❏ Religious Studies (except Theological Professions)
- ❏ Remedial Education
- ❏ Research, Operations
- ❏ Restaurant Management
- ❏ Rhetoric
- ❏ ROTC (Reserve Officers Training Corps)
- ❏ Russian
- ❏ Russian and Slavic Studies
- ❏ Sanitary Engineering
- ❏ Scandinavian Languages
- ❏ Science Education
- ❏ Sculpture
- ❏ Secondary Education, General
- ❏ Secretarial Studies
- ❏ Securities
- ❏ Seismology
- ❏ Semantics
- ❏ Slavic Languages (except Russian)
- ❏ Slavic Studies
- ❏ Social Foundations (History and Philosophy of Education)
- ❏ Social Psychology
- ❏ Social Sciences, General
- ❏ Social Work and Helping Services (except Clinical)
- ❏ Social Work, Clinical
- ❏ Sociology
- ❏ Soil Conservation
- ❏ Soil Management
- ❏ Soils Science (Management and Conservation)
- ❏ South Asian Studies
- ❏ Southeast Asian Studies
- ❏ Spanish
- ❏ Special Education Administration
- ❏ Special Education, General
- ❏ Special Learning Disabilities
- ❏ Speech Correction
- ❏ Speech, Debate, and Forensic Science
- ❏ Speech Pathology and Audiology
- ❏ Statistics and Research, Educational
- ❏ Statistics, Business
- ❏ Statistics in Psychology
- ❏ Statistics, Mathematical and Theoretical
- ❏ Student Personnel (Guidance and Counseling)
- ❏ Systems Analysis
- ❏ Systems and Information Sciences
- ❏ Teaching English as a Foreign Language
- ❏ Technical Education
- ❏ Technologies, Agriculture and Forestry
- ❏ Technologies, Dental
- ❏ Technologies, Engineering
- ❏ Technologies, Medical Laboratory
- ❏ Technologies, Radiologic
- ❏ Technology, Food Science
- ❏ Television
- ❏ Textile Engineering
- ❏ Textiles
- ❏ Theological Professions, General
- ❏ Therapy, Occupational
- ❏ Therapy, Physical
- ❏ Toxicology
- ❏ Transportation and Public Utilities
- ❏ Transportation Engineering
- ❏ Urban Architecture
- ❏ Urban Studies
- ❏ Utilities, Public
- ❏ Vegetable Production

- ❏ Veterinary Medicine (D.V.M.)
- ❏ Veterinary Medicine Specialties (beyond D.V.M.)
- ❏ Vocational Education
- ❏ Weaving
- ❏ West European Studies
- ❏ Wildlife Management
- ❏ Writing, Creative
- ❏ Zoology, General

Now reread the items that you checked. Are there any patterns, such as interest areas, work values, or necessary abilities in common? Complete the following to help you identify patterns in your choices if they exist.

1. Record any of the majors that are science- or math-related (e.g., biology, environmental engineering, statistics).

_____

_____

2. Record any of the majors that are oriented toward the social sciences (e.g., psychology, business, criminology).

_____

_____

3. Record any of the majors that incorporate business practices (e.g., computer science, economics, consumer affairs).

_____

_____

4. Record any of the majors that lead to occupations primarily performed outdoors (e.g., forestry, horticulture).

_____

_____

5. Record any of the majors that lead to occupations that provide high salaries (e.g., medicine, finance).

_____

_____

6. Record any of the majors that require a technical degree (e.g., forest technology, engineering technology).

_____

_____

7. Record any of the majors that require a professional or graduate degree (e.g., law, dentistry).

_____

_____

8. Record any other patterns apparent from your choices (e.g., interest areas, work values, necessary abilities).

_____

_____

Which areas of study would you like to explore at this point? Identify at least three.

_____

_____

_____

Why are you attracted to these majors?

_____

_____

_____

_____

ACTIVITY: IDENTIFYING MAJORS AT YOUR INSTITUTION

In the previous activity, you looked at all areas of study. Now you will narrow these down to only a few realistic undergraduate majors. Obtain a complete list of undergraduate majors available at your institution from your college bulletin, through your institution's Web site, or from your instructor. In exploring college majors, you will not be able to examine details about every educational opportunity, so you must be selective in your approach. From the list of majors available at your institution, identify at least three that interest you.

_____   _____   _____

Review your responses from the previous activity (p. 31–38). Which patterns are evident from the majors you selected from your institution's list?

_____

_____

_____

_____

ACTIVITY: EXAMINING MAJORS BY INTEREST AREA

Examine the majors categorized within the general interest areas listed below and place a check beside each major that holds some interest for you. Note that these are sample majors from the HEGIS list introduced earlier. Also note that a major may appear in more than one interest area; this demonstrates the diversity of interests to which one major may appeal. For additional majors, consult the HEGIS list or your institution's list of majors, and feel free to add alternatives to the examples given here.

Engineering/Technical

- ❏ Agriculture Technologies
- ❏ Architecture
- ❏ Aviation
- ❏ Chemical Engineering
- ❏ Computer Science
- ❏ Electrical Engineering
- ❏ Forest Technology
- ❏ Industrial Technology Education
- ❏ Mechanical Engineering
- ❏ Medical Technology
- ❏ Nuclear Engineering
- ❏ Radiology Technology

Arts/Humanities

- ❏ Advertising
- ❏ American Studies
- ❏ Applied Design
- ❏ Architecture
- ❏ Art Education
- ❏ Art History
- ❏ Art—Painting, Drawing, Sculpture
- ❏ Ceramics
- ❏ Classics
- ❏ Comparative Literature
- ❏ Dance
- ❏ English
- ❏ Ethnic Studies
- ❏ Fashion Design
- ❏ Foreign Languages and Literature
- ❏ History
- ❏ Interior Design
- ❏ Linguistics
- ❏ Music
- ❏ Philosophy
- ❏ Photography
- ❏ Religious Studies
- ❏ Theater

Science

- ❏ Agronomy
- ❏ Astronomy
- ❏ Atmospheric Science and Meteorology
- ❏ Biology
- ❏ Clothing and Textiles
- ❏ Computer Science
- ❏ Dietetics
- ❏ Earth Sciences
- ❏ Fish, Game, and Wildlife Management
- ❏ Food Science and Nutrition
- ❏ Forestry
- ❏ Geography
- ❏ Geology
- ❏ Horticulture
- ❏ Human Nutrition
- ❏ Mathematics
- ❏ Physics
- ❏ Science and Math Education
- ❏ Statistics
- ❏ Zoology

Human Services/Social Sciences

- ❏ Anthropology
- ❏ Audiology
- ❏ Business
- ❏ Child Development
- ❏ Communication
- ❏ Criminology
- ❏ Dental Hygiene
- ❏ Economics
- ❏ Education (all teaching majors)
- ❏ Family Relations
- ❏ Geography
- ❏ Guidance and Counseling
- ❏ Journalism
- ❏ Nursing
- ❏ Occupational Therapy

❏ Physical Therapy
❏ Political Science
❏ Psychology
❏ Recreation
❏ Social Work
❏ Sociology

(In the next following lists, some of the business majors are both people- and data-oriented. However, as is reflected in the coursework, a business major typically places more emphasis on either people or data.)

Business/People-Oriented

❏ Advertising
❏ Consumer Economics
❏ Educational Administration
❏ Fashion Merchandising
❏ Hospital and Health Care Management
❏ Hotel and Restaurant Management
❏ Insurance
❏ International Business

❏ Labor and Industrial Relations
❏ Marketing
❏ Public Relations
❏ Real Estate
❏ Tax Accounting

Business/Data-Oriented

❏ Accounting
❏ Agricultural Economics
❏ Aviation Management
❏ Banking and Finance
❏ City and Regional Planning
❏ Computer Science
❏ Consumer Economics
❏ Hospital Administration
❏ Hotel and Restaurant Management
❏ Insurance
❏ International Business
❏ Natural Resources Management
❏ Parks and Recreation Management
❏ Production Management

Which different interest areas are represented by your major choices?

_____

_____

Which one or two interest areas are best represented by your major choices?

_____

_____

_____

Identify three majors that have emerged from this interest activity.

_____   _____   _____

ACTIVITY: SYNTHESIZING YOUR PERSPECTIVES ON ACADEMIC ALTERNATIVES

Thus far you have identified potential majors using three different methods. Record below the results of each of these approaches.

HEGIS Areas of Study (p. 31–38)	Undergraduate Majors at Your Institution (p. 38)	Majors by Interest Area (p. 39–40)
_____	_____	_____
_____	_____	_____
_____	_____	_____
_____	_____	_____
_____	_____	_____

Do any majors appear on all three lists? On two lists? Write them below.

_____

_____

Are two or more listed under any particular career interest areas? Which ones?

_____

_____

Record the majors you are ready to explore in more detail at this point.

_____

_____

EXPLORING YOUR ACADEMIC ALTERNATIVES

Now that you have identified a few academic career paths in which you have some interest, you can begin to explore each of them in more depth. The activities in this section will help you examine your academic history to see how well prepared you are for the majors you have selected and how your past academic credits will work toward graduation requirements in these majors. You will also learn where to look for outside information that should shed more light on which specific major is right for you.

ACTIVITY: ANALYZING YOUR ACADEMIC TRANSCRIPT

Your past coursework can give you another perspective on the majors you are exploring. If you have had at least one term of school for which you have received grades, obtain a copy of your academic transcript. You will need to learn how to interpret it, as prospective employers may ask for information contained in it; each institution has its own method of writing a transcript.

Based on your transcript or your academic record thus far, answer the following questions:

1. How many credit hours do you have to date?

_____

_____

2. In which subjects did you earn your best grades? Why?

_____

_____

3. In which subjects did you earn your poorest grades? Why?

_____

_____

_____

4. Which subjects did you enjoy the most? Other than a good teacher, why did you enjoy them?

_____

_____

5. Can you determine some academic strengths from examining your transcripts?

_____

_____

6. Does your transcript reveal some academic weaknesses?

_____

_____

7. How would you explain these weaknesses to another person?

_____

_____

8. Overall, do you see any patterns in your academic record that would indicate certain interests, strengths, or limitations for certain majors? What do you think is the reason underlying these patterns?

_____

_____

9. Are there any discrepancies between the majors you are considering and your grades in certain subjects? Describe them.

_____

_____

It is important that the questions you have answered about your past academic work be considered realistically as you begin to narrow your options. (In Unit 6 you will use your transcript again to tentatively create a graduation plan.)

You are now ready to gather solid information about the major(s) you have identified from the previous activities.

Other Resources for Exploring Academic Alternatives

There are many sources for gathering further information about academic fields. Select one or more of the major alternatives you have identified and explore them in more depth through some or all of these avenues:

1. *Self-information.* A realistic assessment of your academic abilities will be helpful here. Consider your past experiences, including your academic preparation and your interest in certain academic fields.
2. *First-hand experience.* Taking a course or two in the area you are considering will give you a very good idea whether this field is for you. You can also do volunteer or part-time work in an area relating to your major. If you are unable to volunteer or otherwise find work in the field, see if you can get permission to observe someone who actually works at a job you are interested in exploring.
3. *Printed materials.* Your institution has a wealth of printed information for you to consult to find out more about your academic field. Your college bulletin contains course descriptions that are especially helpful in describing upper-level courses. The major department has materials on the major, including curriculum sheets. The career planning office will also have materials you can check.
4. *Computerized information systems.* Another excellent source of information is computer systems such as Discover and SIGI-PLUS that offer extensive, up-to-date information about the occupations to which a particular major can lead. Your instructor can inform you which systems are available on your campus.
5. *Internet.* As described in Unit Two, one of the most useful and accessible sources of information is the Internet. Many Web sites provide opportunities to assess your personal characteristics (i.e., interests, abilities, values) and to explore educational and occupational information. Two excellent examples are the Department of Labor's Web site for *O'NET* (http://www.doleta.gov/programs/onet)

that gives information about many specific features of various occupations (including educational requirements), and the Web site for the *Occupational Outlook Handbook* (www.bls.gov/oco) that provides detailed information about more than 250 occupations, and their educational requirements. Your instructor can suggest other Web sites to explore for personal, educational, and occupational information. (Note: As with any source of information, care must be taken to evaluate the accuracy and timeliness of the information provided through the Internet.)

6. *Interviews.*   Faculty members, advisers, college counselors, students enrolled in a major, and alumni who graduated with it—all are potential sources of information about this academic field. Interview guidelines and summary worksheets are provided for you on the pages that follow.

ACTIVITY: ACADEMIC MAJOR INFORMATION SEARCH

Select one or more majors from your list and research them through your college bulletin, faculty, departmental offices, an academic advisor, or your institution's Web site. Record the information you find in the summary sections that follow. As you gather information about them, keep an eye out for key terms related to the major that you can use in the next activity, Computer Research.

Major Information Summary 1:

Major: _____

Sources of information: _____

1. Department or unit where this major can be found:

   _____

2. What basic or general education courses are required for this major (e.g., English, math, social sciences, science, humanities)?

   _____

   _____

3. What basic courses in this major could you take to determine if your interests and abilities match?

   _____

4. Examine the upper level courses listed in the catalog (junior and senior) that are required for this major. List some that sound interesting to you. (Give course numbers and names.)

   _____

   _____

5. What is the *total* number of credit hours needed to graduate with this major? _____
   What is the number of required credit hours for the major itself? _____

6. What is required to enter this major (e.g., certain courses completed, application to a selective admissions area, certain grade point average, no requirements)?

   _____

   _____

7. Other pertinent information about this major:

   _____

   _____

Major Information Summary 2:

Major: _____

Sources of information: _____

1. Department or unit where this major can be found:

   _____

2. What basic or general education courses are required for this major (e.g., English, math, social sciences, science, humanities)?

   _____

   _____

3. What basic courses in this major could you take to determine if your interests and abilities match?

   _____

   _____

4. Examine the upper level courses listed in the catalog (junior and senior) that are required for this major. List some that sound interesting to you. (Give course numbers and names.)

   _____

   _____

5. What is the *total* number of credit hours needed to graduate with this major? _____
   What is the number of required credit hours for the major itself? _____

6. What is required to enter this major (e.g., certain courses completed, application to a selective admissions area, certain grade point average, no requirements)?

   _____

   _____

7. Other pertinent information about this major:

_____

_____

After you have gathered information about the major in which you are most interested, understanding some occupational relationships may help you decide to continue to explore this area. The following activity will guide you through that process.

ACTIVITY: COMPUTER OCCUPATIONAL RESEARCH

To explore possible occupational/career opportunities to which this major may lead, use the resources on the Internet to complete the following activity.

Make a list of key search terms that will be helpful in executing a search on a computerized information system or the World Wide Web. Some on your list might be *career, education, business,* or more specific terms such as the name of the occupation or major (e.g., *public relations, accounting*).

_____   _____   _____

_____   _____   _____

_____   _____   _____

_____   _____   _____

Once you have a list of key terms, find out which systems are available on your campus and how to use them—your instructor, a librarian, or an assistant at the computer center should be able to help you get started. Summarize what you learn on the Computer Occupational Research Summaries that follow. Record what you learn about the occupations to which the majors you have selected can lead. Add your own questions to the summary sheet if they do not appear there already.

Computer Occupational Research Summary

Major 1: _____

Computer Resource Used (e.g., Internet site, Discover, SIGI-PLUS, other): _____

Occupation 1 to which this major may lead: _____

  1. Education/training required: _____

_____

  2. Skills required: _____

_____

3. Some tasks involved in the work: _____

_____

4. Personal satisfactions: _____

_____

5. Employment outlook: _____

_____

6. Other information: _____

_____

Occupation 2 to which this major may lead: _____

1. Education/training required: _____

_____

2. Skills required: _____

_____

3. Some tasks involved in the work: _____

_____

4. Personal satisfactions: _____

_____

5. Employment outlook: _____

_____

6. Other information: _____

_____

Computer Occupational Research Summary

Major 2: _____

Computer Resource Used (e.g., Internet site, Discover, SIGI-PLUS, other): _____

Occupation 1 to which this major may lead: _____

1. Education/training required: _____

_____

2. Skills required: _____

_____

3. Some tasks involved in the work: _____

_____

4. Personal satisfactions: _____

_____

5. Employment outlook: _____

_____

6. Other information: _____

_____

Occupation 2 to which this major may lead: _____

1. Education/training required: _____

_____

2. Skills required: _____

_____

3. Some tasks involved in the work: _____

_____

4. Personal satisfactions: _____

_____

5. Employment outlook: _____

_____

6. Other information: _____

_____

ACTIVITY: INTERVIEWING OTHERS

One of your most valuable sources of information about the majors you are exploring is people who are knowledgeable about those areas. Locate at least two people who are familiar with the majors you are exploring—faculty members, academic advisers, or other students in the major—and arrange to interview them. Before the interview, write in the following spaces some of the questions you would like to ask. Take notes during your interviews in the space provided here. Then complete the Interview Summary sheets on the following pages to record what you learned. Add your own questions to the summary sheets if they do not appear there already.

Sample questions to get you started:

- Why do students select this major?
- What basic education courses would you recommend I take for this major?
- How much flexibility does this program have?
- What elective courses would be helpful?
- What are some other sources of information about this major?
- What kind of campus activities or student organizations on campus relate to this major?
- Does this major require or is it desirable to have a graduate degree in this area?
- What kind of careers are possible with this major after graduation?

Your questions about specific majors:

Major: _____

1. _____

2. _____

3. _____

4. _____

Major: _____

1. _____

2. _____

3. _____

4. _____

Your interview notes:

_____

_____

_____

_____

_____

_____

Interview Summary: Academic Major

Major: _____

Interviewee: _____

Title: _____

Department: _____

1. Prior to this interview, what were your assumptions about this major field of study?

_____

_____

2. What important aspects of this major did you discuss? Why are these important?

_____

_____

3. What did you learn about the course requirements for this major?

_____

_____

_____

4. What are some positive aspects of this major? Negative aspects?

_____

_____

5. What did you learn about potential career opportunities in this area of study?

_____

_____

6. Based on the information you received in this interview, would you pursue this as a major? Why or why not?

_____

_____

7. What was your overall impression of the interview?

_____

_____

Interview Summary: Academic Major

Major: _____

Interviewee: _____

Title: _____

Department: _____

1. Prior to this interview, what were your assumptions about this major field of study?

_____

_____

2. What important aspects of this major did you discuss? Why are these important?

_____

_____

3. What did you learn about the course requirements for this major?

_____

_____

4. What are some positive aspects of this major? Negative aspects?

_____

_____

5. What did you learn about potential career opportunities in this area of study?

_____

_____

6. Based on the information you received in this interview, would you pursue this as a major? Why or why not?

_____

_____

7. What was your overall impression of the interview?

_____

_____

SUMMARY

In this unit, you identified several academic alternatives that might interest you to some degree. You then explored these possible majors in more depth through several avenues of research. Now that you know more about the majors you chose to explore, what do you see as the pros and cons of each?

Major	Pros	Cons
_____	_____	_____
_____	_____	_____
_____	_____	_____
_____	_____	_____

List at least two or three majors that are the most interesting to you at this point.

_____

_____

CASE STUDY: MARIA

Maria entered college undecided because she wasn't sure what was involved in different majors, such as coursework or jobs to which they might lead. She knew she was interested in the health professions, but she wasn't sure if she had the patience or the science background to succeed in any of them. She had volunteered in a hospital during high school and had enjoyed that work environment. Right now her strongest interests are in nursing, physical therapy, and pharmacy.

What information does Maria need in order to narrow her options? What more information do you need?

_____

_____

_____

Where can she obtain this information? Where can you find this information?

_____

_____

_____

What specific action can you take now to move along in the process of deciding about a major?

_____

_____

_____

CASE STUDY: DUANE

When Duane entered college he was sure he wanted to be an engineer. He performed above average in math and science classes in high school, and his family always encouraged him to be an engineer. Duane is taking engineering-related courses during his freshman year, but is not enjoying them. Although he is studying constantly, he isn't doing very well in the core courses. He is not sure he would enjoy the type of work in which engineers are involved and realizes he knew very little about engineering when he chose it initially. Duane is becoming very discouraged and is considering a major change. He is getting his best grades in economics and English and enjoys both subjects very much. He hasn't discussed his situation with anyone, but he feels pressured to do something about it before he schedules courses for his sophomore year.

What kind of information does Duane need in order to decide about a change of major? What kind do you need?

_____

_____

_____

Where can he obtain this information? Where can you?

_____

_____

_____

What specific action can you take now to move along in the process?

_____

_____

_____

PERSONAL LOG #3

Record your thoughts and feelings about what you learned through exploring your different major alternatives in this unit. (For example, how does the self-information you gathered in Unit Two match the majors you identified in this unit? Do you have any possible future occupations in mind that will help you select a major?)

_____

_____

_____

_____

_____

_____

_____

_____

_____

_____

_____

_____

_____

_____

_____

_____

_____

_____

_____

_____

Mid-Course Instructor Interview

Make an appointment with your course instructor after you complete Unit Two or Three. List the concerns and questions you have at this point. Take this sheet and your transcript with you when you meet with your instructor.

1. _____

_____

2. _____

_____

3. _____

_____

4. _____

_____

5. _____

_____

6. _____

_____

UNIT FOUR
Exploring Occupations

Your true pilot cares nothing about anything
on earth but the river, and his pride in his
occupation surpasses the pride of kings.
                                                    Mark Twain

ONCE YOU HAVE MADE a decision about one or two academic directions to in-
vestigate, you need to examine the occupations that might be available to you if you
graduate with one of these choices as your major. In this unit you will explore some
of these occupational possibilities.

Possible future occupation can impact your choice of major in two different ways. You
can select a major directly related to an occupation, requiring specific skills for a specific
job, such as physical therapy, electrical engineering, or elementary education. Alterna-
tively, you can choose a major that provides more of a general preparation for the work

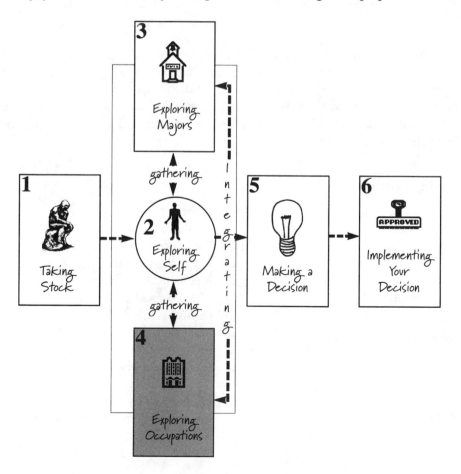

world and can give entry into a variety of professions, such as history, literature, or philosophy. You will be able to examine academic–occupational relationships through both of these perspectives in this unit.

SELECTING YOUR OCCUPATIONAL ALTERNATIVES

In Unit Two you assessed your personal interests and strengths through six career areas. In Unit Three you examined academic majors through these same six areas and other criteria. This unit will assist you in making connections between some academic majors you are considering and occupational fields that might relate directly or indirectly, based on these same career areas.

ACTIVITY: IDENTIFYING OCCUPATIONS BY CAREER AREA

List below some majors you are now seriously considering based on the information you gathered in Units Two and Three, and indicate the career areas within which they can be found.

Major   **Career Area**

_____   _____

_____   _____

_____   _____

Now examine the following list of occupations, which is organized by the career areas you experienced in Units Two and Three. Some occupations might appear in more than one career area because worker interests and skills might be relevant in a related field. Check all the occupations that are interesting to you. (More complete lists of occupations can be obtained from the publications and Web sites of the U.S. Department of Labor, such as the *Occupational Outlook Handbook* at http://www.bls.gov/oco and *o*net* [formerly the *Dictionary of Occupational Titles*] at http://onetcenter.org.)

Engineering/Technical

- ❏ Agricultural Educator
- ❏ Animal Breeder or Trainer
- ❏ Animal Nutritionist
- ❏ Aviator
- ❏ Beekeeper
- ❏ Computer Software Engineer
- ❏ Computer Data Systems Analyst
- ❏ Construction Engineer
- ❏ Dental Technologist
- ❏ Electrical Engineer
- ❏ Electronics Technician
- ❏ Environmental Designer
- ❏ Fish and Wildlife Manager
- ❏ Fish Farmer
- ❏ Fitness Trainer

- ❏ Forester
- ❏ Geologist
- ❏ Industrial Arts Teacher
- ❏ Industrial Engineer
- ❏ Mechanical Engineer
- ❏ Metallurgical Engineer
- ❏ Oceanographer
- ❏ Photographer, Scientific
- ❏ Prosthetist
- ❏ Radiologic Technologist
- ❏ Turf Manager
- ❏ Virtual Reality Designer
- ❏ Vocational Agriculture Teacher
- ❏ Welding Engineer
- ❏ Wildlife Manager

Arts/Humanities

- ❑ Account Executive
- ❑ Actor
- ❑ Architect
- ❑ Archivist
- ❑ Art Teacher
- ❑ Artist
- ❑ Bilingual Educator
- ❑ Book Editor
- ❑ Cartoonist
- ❑ Choral Director
- ❑ Copywriter
- ❑ Critic
- ❑ Dance Therapist
- ❑ Digital Graphic Designer
- ❑ Drama Teacher
- ❑ English Teacher
- ❑ Equestrian
- ❑ Film Editor
- ❑ Graphic Designer
- ❑ Historian
- ❑ Instrumental Musician
- ❑ Interior Designer
- ❑ Interpreter
- ❑ Landscape Architect
- ❑ Linguist
- ❑ Literary Agent
- ❑ Model
- ❑ Music Director
- ❑ Music Teacher
- ❑ News Editor
- ❑ Newspaper Editor
- ❑ Orchestra Conductor
- ❑ Painter
- ❑ Philologist
- ❑ Photojournalist
- ❑ Printmaker
- ❑ Scientific Editor
- ❑ Sculptor
- ❑ Translator

Science

- ❑ Actuary
- ❑ Aeronautical Engineer
- ❑ Aerospace Scientist
- ❑ Agricultural Engineer
- ❑ Agronomist
- ❑ Airplane Pilot
- ❑ Anatomist
- ❑ Animal Pathologist
- ❑ Animal Psychologist
- ❑ Animal Scientist
- ❑ Anthropologist
- ❑ Archeologist
- ❑ Astronomer
- ❑ Audiologist
- ❑ Biochemist
- ❑ Biologist
- ❑ Biomedical Engineer
- ❑ Botanist
- ❑ Cell Biologist
- ❑ Ceramic Engineer
- ❑ Chemical Engineer
- ❑ Chemist
- ❑ City and Regional Planner
- ❑ Civil Engineer
- ❑ Computer Scientist
- ❑ Criminalist
- ❑ Dentist
- ❑ Educational Psychologist
- ❑ Electrical Engineer
- ❑ Entomologist
- ❑ Environmental Engineer
- ❑ Experimental Psychologist
- ❑ Food Technologist
- ❑ Forest Technologist
- ❑ General Practitioner
- ❑ Geneticist
- ❑ Geographer
- ❑ Geologist
- ❑ Horticulturist
- ❑ Industrial Arts Teacher
- ❑ Industrial Technology Educator
- ❑ Information Scientist
- ❑ Marine Biologist
- ❑ Mathematician
- ❑ Medical Technologist
- ❑ Metallurgist
- ❑ Microbiologist
- ❑ Neuroscientist
- ❑ Nuclear Engineer
- ❑ Nurse Anesthetist
- ❑ Optometrist
- ❑ Osteopathic Physician
- ❑ Pathologist
- ❑ Perfusionist
- ❑ Pharmacist
- ❑ Pharmacy Technician
- ❑ Physician
- ❑ Physician Assistant

- ❏ Plant Pathologist
- ❏ Psychiatrist
- ❏ Psychometrician
- ❏ Sociologist
- ❏ Soil Conservationist
- ❏ Statistician
- ❏ Surgeon
- ❏ Systems Analyst
- ❏ Toxicologist
- ❏ Veterinarian
- ❏ Zoologist

Human Services/Social Sciences

- ❏ Academic Dean
- ❏ Adult Education Teacher
- ❏ Athletic Director
- ❏ Athletic Trainer
- ❏ Clergy Member
- ❏ Clinical Psychologist
- ❏ Clinical Sociologist
- ❏ Coach
- ❏ College Teacher
- ❏ Counseling Psychologist
- ❏ Criminologist
- ❏ Dental Hygienist
- ❏ Detective
- ❏ Dietitian
- ❏ Elementary Teacher
- ❏ Executive Chef
- ❏ Family Counselor
- ❏ Geographer
- ❏ Head Coach
- ❏ Historian
- ❏ Home Economist
- ❏ Industrial Psychologist
- ❏ Librarian
- ❏ Managing Editor
- ❏ Motion Picture Director
- ❏ Nurse
- ❏ Occupational Therapist
- ❏ Park Naturalist
- ❏ Philologist
- ❏ Physical Education Teacher
- ❏ Physical Therapist
- ❏ Podiatrist
- ❏ Police Officer
- ❏ Political Scientist
- ❏ Preschool Teacher
- ❏ Public Health Educator

- ❏ Recreation Leader
- ❏ Recreation Therapist
- ❏ Research Analyst
- ❏ Residence Counselor
- ❏ Respiratory Therapist
- ❏ School Nurse
- ❏ Secondary School Teacher
- ❏ Social Worker
- ❏ Special Education Teacher
- ❏ Speech Pathologist
- ❏ Speech–Hearing Therapist
- ❏ Welfare Director

Business/People-Oriented

- ❏ Airport Manager
- ❏ Athletic Manager
- ❏ Business Manager
- ❏ Buyer
- ❏ Campus Director
- ❏ College Department Head
- ❏ Dietitian
- ❏ Director of Admissions
- ❏ Director of Counseling
- ❏ Director of Institutional Research
- ❏ Fashion Coordinator
- ❏ Financial Planner
- ❏ Flight Attendant
- ❏ Genealogist
- ❏ Head Coach
- ❏ Hotel and Restaurant Manager
- ❏ Judge
- ❏ Labor Relations Manager
- ❏ Lawyer
- ❏ Manager
- ❏ Model
- ❏ Newscaster
- ❏ Producer
- ❏ Public Relations Representative
- ❏ Records Analysis Manager
- ❏ Reporter
- ❏ Salesperson
- ❏ Sales Representative
- ❏ Social Welfare Administrator
- ❏ Sports Instructor
- ❏ Tax Attorney
- ❏ Travel Agent
- ❏ Urban Planner
- ❏ Vice President

Business/Data-Oriented

❑ Accountant
❑ Banker
❑ Business Educator
❑ City Planner
❑ Computer Support Specialist
❑ Cost Accountant
❑ Data Processor
❑ Desktop Publisher

❑ Entrepreneur
❑ Environmental Analyst
❑ Financial Analyst
❑ Medical Records Administrator
❑ Medical Secretary
❑ Production Manager
❑ Systems Accountant
❑ Tax Preparer

Review the checked items and pick at least three occupations in which you are interested.

Occupation	**Career Area**

How do these occupations relate to the majors you identified in Unit Three?

_____

_____

_____

Which majors and occupations are in the same career area?

_____

_____

_____

Have you identified any occupations that are in career areas *not* represented by your major choices? If so, what are they?

_____

If they are in occupations in which you have a strong interest and the ability to perform the tasks needed, you might wish to reexamine the list of majors in that career area. Are there majors not on your list that you might want to examine? If so, which ones?

_____

_____

Which majors that are of interest to you have a *direct* relationship to an occupation (e.g., physical therapy, architecture)?

Major	**Occupation**
_____	_____
_____	_____
_____	_____

Which majors on your list have *no* direct relationship to an occupation but are general preparation for many career fields?

_____

_____

_____

As you explore academic–occupational relationships, you will discover that not all college majors appear to lead directly to a specific occupation. However, all college majors do lead to a college degree, which is essential for obtaining a job in many cases. Indeed, surveys indicate that many people work in jobs for which the college degree itself is the most important prerequisite. People often are trained "on the job" to perform the tasks for which they are hired. Thus, even majors that do not provide specific skills are of value in the job market.

The Appendix on pages 97–107 offers some tips for making yourself marketable when you are searching for employment.

Now that you have identified some occupations that interest you, the next step is to gather information about those occupations so that you can base your major and occupational decisions on data that is solid, realistic, and current. The next section contains information about where to gather this information and helps you frame the questions that will lead to a greater understanding of these occupations.

EXPLORING YOUR OCCUPATIONAL ALTERNATIVES

In Unit Three you explored your academic alternatives in more depth. You will now use some of the same techniques to explore in more detail the occupations you just listed. During this exploration process keep in mind that the relationship between your academic major and your future occupation varies depending on the field. Some majors will prepare you for one specific occupation, such as physical therapy, landscape architecture, or chemical engineering. Other majors are not so directly, linked to one occupation, instead preparing you for the work force in general and leading indirectly to a variety of fields. For example, a major in English might lead to a job in publishing or business or many other fields. Also, in some cases, you can prepare for a specific occupation with any of several majors. For example, you may want a career in public relations after graduation; a degree in any major for which writing skills and general business knowledge are emphasized can lead you to your goal.

There are several sources for discovering further information about occupational fields. Select one or more of the alternatives you have identified and explore them in more depth through some or all of these avenues:

1. *Self-information.* A realistic assessment of your academic abilities will be helpful here. Consider your past experiences, including your academic preparation and your interest in certain academic fields.

2. *First-hand experience.* Internships or volunteer or part-time work in this occupation will give you a good perspective on whether you enjoy this type of work. If you are unable to volunteer or otherwise find work in the field, see if you can get permission to observe someone who actually works at a job you are interested in exploring.

3. *The Internet.* As indicated previously, the Internet has revolutionized the access to and the availability and exploration of career information. In addition to government Web sites already cited, the number and type of career-related Web sites offer interactive experiences to gather personal, educational, and occupational information (e.g., http://www.iseek.org; http://www.keirsey.com; http://www.collegeview.com).

4. *Printed materials.* Your library has a wealth of printed information for you to consult to find out more about your occupational field. Your campus career services office will also have materials you can check.

5. *Computerized information systems.* Another excellent source of information is computer systems such as DISCOVER and SIGI-PLUS that offer extensive, up-to-date information about the occupations in which you are interested. Your instructor can tell you which systems are available on your campus.

6. *Interviews.* Anyone who works in your field of interest is a potential source of information about the field. Interview guidelines and summary worksheets are provided for you on the pages that follow.

ACTIVITY: OCCUPATIONAL RESEARCH

Select one or more occupations from your list and research it using materials you find in the career planning office and the library. Record the information you find on the research summaries that follow. Add your own questions to the summary sheet if they do not appear there already.

Make a list of key search terms that will be helpful in executing a search on a computerized information system or the World Wide Web. Some words on your list might be *career, education,* or *business,* or more specific terms such as the name of the occupation or major (e.g., *public relations, accounting*).

_____	_____	_____
_____	_____	_____
_____	_____	_____
_____	_____	_____

Once you have a list of key terms, find out which systems are available on your campus and how to use them; your instructor, a librarian, or an assistant at the computer center should be able to help you get started. For example, remember when Sabrina (p. 26) explored her interest in sports? She did that by accessing the *Occupational Outlook Handbook* (http://www.bls.gov/oco) and scrolling through the alphabetical listing of occupations under the "Professional and Related Occupational Cluster." Once she discovered "Athletes, Coaches, Umpires, and Related Workers," Sabrina was able to read about various sports-related occupations, their working conditions, salaries, educational requirements, and many other interesting facts.

Occupation Description

Occupation 1: _____

Sources of information: _____

1. Nature of work:

   _____

   _____

2. Working conditions:

   _____

   _____

3. Education or training required for this work:

   _____

   _____

4. Related academic majors:

   _____

   _____

5. Employment outlook for this occupation:

   _____

   _____

6. Salary range for this occupation:

   _____

   _____

7. Related occupations:

   _____

   _____

Occupation Description

Occupation 2: _____

Sources of information: _____

1. Nature of work:

   _____

   _____

2. Working conditions:

   _____

   _____

3. Education or training required for this work:

   _____

   _____

4. Related academic majors:

   _____

   _____

5. Employment outlook for this occupation:

   _____

   _____

6. Salary range for this occupation:

   _____

   _____

7. Related occupations:

   _____

   _____

ACTIVITY: INTERVIEWING OTHERS

One of your most valuable sources of information about the occupations you are exploring is people who are knowledgeable about those areas. Locate at least two people who work in or are familiar with the occupations you are exploring and arrange to interview them. Before the interview, write in the spaces below some of the questions you would like to ask. Take notes during your interviews in the space provided below. Then complete the Interview Summary on the following pages to record what you learned. Add your own questions to the Interview Summary if they do not appear there already.

Your questions about specific occupations:

Occupation: _____

1. _____

2. _____

3. _____

4. _____

Occupation: _____

1. _____

2. _____

3. _____

4. _____

Your interview notes:

_____

_____

_____

_____

_____

_____

_____

Interview Summary: Occupational Area

Occupational Area: _____

Interviewee: _____

Title: _____

Place of Employment: _____

1. Prior to this interview, what were your assumptions about this career area?

   _____

   _____

2. What important aspects of this career area did you discuss? Why are these important?

   _____

   _____

3. What does this worker like about this career area?

   _____

   _____

4. What does this worker dislike about this career area?

   _____

   _____

5. Is this occupational area compatible with your work values? (p. 22–23)

   _____

   _____

6. What majors or training might lead you to this career?

   _____

   _____

7. What are three things you learned about this career area?

   _____

   _____

8. Based on the information you received in this interview, would you pursue this as a career area? Why or why not?

   _____

   _____

9. What was your overall impression of the interview?

   _____

   _____

Interview Summary: Occupational Area

Occupational Area: _____

Interviewee: _____

Title: _____

Place of Employment: _____

1. Prior to this interview, what were your assumptions about this career area?

   _____

   _____

2. What important aspects of this career area did you discuss? Why are these important?

   _____

   _____

3. What does this worker like about this career area?

   _____

   _____

4. What does this worker dislike about this career area?

   _____

   _____

5. Is this occupational area compatible with your work values? (see pp. 22–23)

   _____

   _____

6. What majors or training might lead you to this career?

   _____

   _____

7. What are three things you learned about this career area?

   _____

   _____

8. Based on the information you received in this interview, would you pursue this as a career area? Why or why not?

   _____

   _____

9. What was your overall impression of the interview?

   _____

   _____

SUMMARY

In this unit, you identified several occupational alternatives that might interest you to some degree. You then explored these possible jobs in more depth through several avenues of research. Now that you know more about the occupations you chose to explore, what do you see as the pros and cons of each?

Occupation	Pros	Cons
_____	_____	_____
_____	_____	_____
_____	_____	_____
_____	_____	_____

List two or three occupations that are still interesting to you at this point.

_____

_____

_____

Which academic majors might help you prepare for these occupations?

Occupation	Major
_____	_____
_____	_____
_____	_____

CASE STUDY: KIM

After careful examination and thought, Kim has decided upon a psychology major. She looked at all the course-work involved, interviewed faculty in the department, and talked with seniors majoring in psychology. She is also thinking about taking business courses to expand her options after graduation. She interviewed several people in the human resources (personnel) side of business who had undergraduate psychology or business majors and found them to be satisfied with both their undergraduate major and career. She then used some Web sites to explore these areas and found that her interests and abilities for both areas were confirmed. She is certain that this is the direction she wants to pursue. What do you think Kim should do next?

_____

_____

_____

_____

_____

PERSONAL LOG #4

Record your thoughts and feelings about what you learned through exploring your different occupational alternatives in this unit. (For example, how does the self-information you gathered in Unit Two match some of the occupations you identified in this unit? How do academic majors you identified in Unit Three relate to these occupations? Did you find possible related occupations that you had not considered before?)

UNIT FIVE
Making a Decision

Once a decision was made, I did not worry
about it afterward.

Harry Truman

YOU HAVE GATHERED a great deal of information about your personal characteristics, academic programs, and occupations. You now need to integrate this information in order to make a realistic and satisfying choice of major. If you are comfortable with the information you have gathered and the alternatives you have identified so far, you are ready to move on to the final phase of making a decision: committing yourself to one of your alternatives.

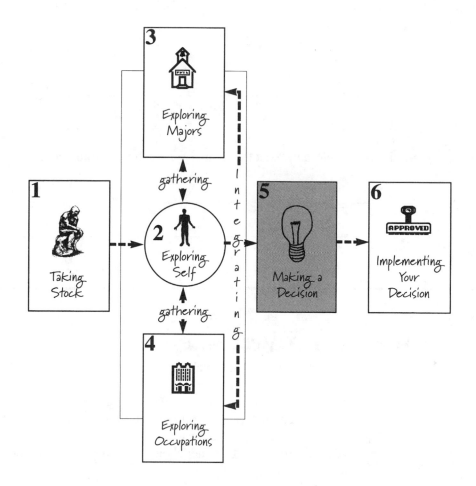

THE DECISION-MAKING PROCESS

Thus far in this book you have assessed your interests and abilities, learned about various academic options, examined your academic record, researched occupational fields relating to majors you are interested in, and perhaps reassessed an earlier decision. The most important part of your task remains: integrating all this information and analyzing it in order to identify a realistic academic choice. Each of the activities in this unit is one step toward completing this task.

ACTIVITY: LOOKING AT YOUR MAJOR CHOICES

List below all the majors you have identified thus far as being both interesting to you and academically attainable by you at your current institution.

Major   **Department, College, or School**

_____   _____

_____   _____

_____   _____

Do these majors have anything in common (e.g., all are social science oriented, all lead to one career area, all are within the same department or college)?

_____

_____

_____

Can you eliminate any of your major alternatives at this point? Why can you eliminate them?

_____

_____

_____

THE ART OF COMPROMISE

Another factor affecting decision making is the art of compromise. If you are undecided, you may not be able to choose between two or more seemingly desirable major or occupational choices. You may not be able to decide because you want the "perfect" choice. If you are changing majors, you also might be looking for the perfect alternative. Compromise is a concession or an agreement to give up a desirable quality in one choice for a desirable quality in another choice. You may have to compromise between two majors, for example, that have equally desirable qualities. Or you may find that a compromise is needed because of some undesirable qualities within a choice.

As you move through the process of making a major choice, keep in mind that there are no black or white, or right or wrong choices. You will be making a decision based on the best information available to you at that time. Developing the ability to compromise during this decision-making process might be required. This might mean examining the pros and cons of each alternative to evaluate the most desirable and un-desirable qualities in each. Later in this unit you will be doing just that.

Consider this need to compromise as you progress through the decision-making activities that follow.

DECISION-MAKING STYLE

On pages 7 and 8 you analyzed your decision-making style. Go back to that activity and determine if you have arrived at this tentative decision spontaneously or systematically. If you tend to be a spontaneous decision maker, it is hoped that this decision "feels right" and that you are ready to make a commitment, knowing that it can be altered or changed in the future. If this choice does not "feel right," you might want to retrace your steps to see what other majors you identified that are similar to this one.

If you are a more systematic decision maker, it is hoped that you are feeling com-fortable with your choice knowing that you arrived at it in a methodical, organized way. If you are having second thoughts about this choice, you might want to retrace your steps to gather more information about other alternatives that you identified along the way.

Do you want to explore another major at this point? If so, which one? _____ Return to the place in this workbook where you think you need more information (e.g., personal assessment, academic ma-jor exploration, occupational information) or need to reengage the process.

ACTIVITY: NARROWING YOUR LIST TO REALISTIC ALTERNATIVES

One important consideration in choosing a major is its relationship to your goals and future occupation. In Unit Two you identified some of your work values. Review these and decide which are the most important ones. Would you like to change any of these values? Also consider any values you identified from other sources (e.g., the Internet Discover, SIGI-PLUS, interviews).

Now record your most important work values in the downward column of blanks along the left-hand side of the chart. In the blanks in the row across the top of the chart, record your occupational alternatives. Wher-ever one of your occupational alternatives fulfills one of your work values, place a check in the corresponding square. For instance, if one of your occupational alternatives is social work, and one of your values is altruism, place a check in the box where these items meet on the chart.

OCCUPATIONAL ALTERNATIVES

Work Values			
_____			
_____			
_____			
_____			
_____			

Review the filled-in chart. Which occupation has the most checks in its column?

_____

_____

_____

How does this occupation relate to the major you are considering?

_____

_____

_____

ACTIVITY: MAKING A TENTATIVE CHOICE

You are now at a point where one major should be clearly more desirable and attainable than the others. Check this major against the other information you now have.

Major: _____

Circle One		**Information**
yes	no	This major matches the interest patterns I identified in Unit Two.
yes	no	Occupations relating to this major are interesting and seem to be within my reach.
yes	no	The work environments that I prefer are in career areas compatible with this major.
yes	no	The work values I identified are incorporated into the occupations related to this major.
yes	no	The courses required for this major interest me.
yes	no	I have the ability to do the coursework for this major.
yes	no	The time it would take to complete this major is acceptable to me.
yes	no	If my major requires selective admission, I know the application procedures needed to be accepted.
yes	no	I currently have the grade point average (gpa) to be accepted in this major. (If "no," is it realistic to expect I can reach this gpa in a reasonable period of time? If not, what are the consequences?)
yes	no	I am more aware now of how I make decisions (how I gather and analyze information) and am comfortable with my "style."
yes	no	I feel good about my choice of major.

Did you answer "yes" to all these questions? If so, you are ready to test your choice against the force field analysis that follows. If not, what was your reason for answering "no" to one or more questions?

_____

_____

_____

_____

_____

_____

_____

_____

_____

_____

_____

_____

_____

_____

ACTIVITY: A FORCE FIELD ANALYSIS OF MY DECISION

Kurt Lewin, a noted psychologist, adapted the concept of force field from the physical sciences to the social sciences. Although you have examined the pros and cons of past choices, the force field analysis goes beyond that basic activity. When using the force field concept, you list the positive forces or reasons (pros) for your choice and negative forces or reasons (cons) against your choice. Now try to move the negative forces (those that are against your choice) from the right side of the line to the positive force field on the left side of the line. To change these negative reasons to positive ones, you must try to take some kind of action to alter them.

When there are more positive reasons for your choice than negative reasons, you have probably made a good one. If there are many more negative reasons than positive ones, you might want to rethink your decision.

The following Case Study demonstrates how a Force Field Analysis worked for a real student.

CASE STUDY: KIM

In Unit Four, Kim decided that she wanted to major in psychology. She checked her choice through a Force Field Analysis.

FORCES FOR (+) A PSYCHOLOGY MAJOR ←	FORCES AGAINST (−) A PSYCHOLOGY MAJOR
Love the psych coursework Get good grades in courses Have wonderful faculty advisor Satisfies my interest in biology Able to assist with lab work Have time in curriculum to take some business courses Compatible with my values of helping people This major is intellectually stimulating	Too many psych majors—crowded courses Not enough time to take extra human resource courses May be difficult to find a job with this major Need a Ph.D. to be a psychologist

Kim found that she had more positive reasons to major in psychology than negative ones. When she examined the negative reasons, some were impossible to move to the positive side. For example, there is nothing she can do about the large number of psych majors, so she will need to accept large and crowded courses. She does not want to stay for an extra semester to take more human resource courses and she is not sure she will ever want to become a psychologist.

On the other hand, she has moved the negative reason about a job to the positive side by working with a career counselor in her campus career planning office. She discovered that psychology majors from her college have successfully entered a wide variety of jobs in many career fields. She is currently developing her job search skills to enhance her chances of obtaining a challenging job after graduation.

Now test your choice of major in a force field analysis

Force Field Analysis of Your New Major

Name of major_____

List the positive forces on the left; list the negative forces on the right.

FORCES (+) FOR MY NEW MAJOR ←	FORCES (−) AGAINST MY NEW MAJOR

Are there more forces for success in your new major than against? If so, you will want to make a commitment to your new major and continue through the remaining activities. If not, consider how you can change the negatives to positives. If you still have more negatives than positives, you may want to return to the previous activities and rework them.

ACTIVITY: COMMITTING TO YOUR NEW MAJOR

Congratulations! You have selected an academic major. Your decision was made on the sound basis of accurate and realistic information about yourself, academic requirements, and occupational options that attract you.

My academic major choice is: _____

It is in the department (or college or school) of: _____

My new major's departmental office is located at: _____

Building	Street

ACTIVITY: PLANNING YOUR ACADEMIC SCHEDULE

You now need to systematically plan future coursework for your degree and learn about the special services on campus that will help you with your job search later. You can obtain a checklist of requirements from the department or from your instructor.

Major: _____

Department: _____

Record below the courses you have already taken to complete the degree requirements for this major. List each course under the area that it fulfills and note the number of credit hours for each.

General Education Requirements			Department or College Requirements			Academic Major Requirements		
Course Title	Credit Hours	Grade	Course Title	Credit Hours	Grade	Course Title	Credit Hours	Grade
_____	_____	_____	_____	_____	_____	_____	_____	_____
_____	_____	_____	_____	_____	_____	_____	_____	_____
_____	_____	_____	_____	_____	_____	_____	_____	_____
_____	_____	_____	_____	_____	_____	_____	_____	_____
_____	_____	_____	_____	_____	_____	_____	_____	_____
_____	_____	_____	_____	_____	_____	_____	_____	_____

General Education Requirements			Department or College Requirements			Academic Major Requirements		
Course Title	Credit Hours	Grade	Course Title	Credit Hours	Grade	Course Title	Credit Hours	Grade
___	___	___	___	___	___	___	___	___
___	___	___	___	___	___	___	___	___
___	___	___	___	___	___	___	___	___
___	___	___	___	___	___	___	___	___
___	___	___	___	___	___	___	___	___
___	___	___	___	___	___	___	___	___
___	___	___	___	___	___	___	___	___

Total number of hours you have earned toward this degree so far: _____

Now list the courses you still need in order to complete this degree. Divide them into the semesters or quarters you plan to take them. If you think you have more than three semesters or quarters left in school, make photocopies of these pages.

Courses

	Department	**Course Number**	**Credit Hours**
1.	___	___	___
2.	___	___	___
3.	___	___	___
4.	___	___	___
5.	___	___	___
6.	___	___	___
7.	___	___	___
8.	___	___	___

Total hours this quarter/semester: _____ Semester/Quarter: (e.g., fall, spring) _____

Cumulative quarter/semester hours: _____ Year: _____

Courses

Department	Course Number	Credit Hours
1. _____	_____	_____
2. _____	_____	_____
3. _____	_____	_____
4. _____	_____	_____
5. _____	_____	_____
6. _____	_____	_____
7. _____	_____	_____
8. _____	_____	_____

Total hours this quarter/semester: _____ Semester/Quarter: _____

Cumulative quarter/semester hours: _____ Year: _____

Courses

Department	Course Number	Credit Hours
1. _____	_____	_____
2. _____	_____	_____
3. _____	_____	_____
4. _____	_____	_____
5. _____	_____	_____
6. _____	_____	_____
7. _____	_____	_____
8. _____	_____	_____

Total hours this quarter/semester: _____ Semester/Quarter: _____

Cumulative quarter/semester hours: _____ Year: _____

How many hours are required to graduate with this major? _____

How many hours do you still need to earn this degree? _____

What are the transfer or entry criteria to the department or college (if any)?

_____

_____

_____

What courses (if any) do you still need to take before you can transfer?

_____

_____

What other requirements, if any, do you still need to complete before you can transfer?

_____

_____

Are you interested in graduate or professional school? If yes, what are your reasons? What area(s) are you considering? What special criteria are there for entering this graduate program?

_____

_____

_____

_____

How do you feel about this major? Are you satisfied with it? Is it realistic and attainable? What courses are you looking forward to taking and why?

_____

_____

_____

_____

ACTIVITY: EXAMINING RELATED JOBS

The relationship between majors and occupations is obvious for some; for others, it is not. In order to explore the relationship between the major you have just selected and work environments to which it may lead, contact your campus career services office.

The career services office for this major is at: _____

Building	Street	Phone Number

Check the job postings at the career services office or other sources (e.g., Internet classifieds). Select two jobs that interest you and answer the following questions.

Job #1 Title and Description

_____

_____

_____

What qualifications are required for this position?

_____

_____

How will you fit these qualifications after you graduate?

_____

_____

Which of your work values can be fulfilled by this position?

_____

_____

_____

Job #2 Title and Description

_____

_____

What qualifications are required for this position?

_____

_____

How will you fit these qualifications after you graduate?

_____

_____

Which of your work values can be fulfilled by this position?

_____

_____

What experiences (e.g., work experience, extracurricular activities, volunteer work) will you need between now and graduation to enhance your chances of obtaining a position such as one of these?

_____

_____

List three companies or institutions where employment opportunities for your specific interests may exist. For listings of such companies, consult your career services office, the Internet for the organization's Web site, the yellow pages, a career library, a computer job bank, and similar sources:

_____

_____

_____

ACTIVITY: ASSESSING YOUR JOB SEARCH SKILLS

Even though you may think graduation and searching for a job after graduation are far away, you will be developing critical workplace knowledge and skills during all of your college years.

Rate your job search skills on the chart below. You need to work on upgrading any skill that you do not rate "excellent." Depending on which skill it is, you might contact your career services office, attend a resume-writing workshop, practice interviewing with a classmate, or explore internship opportunities. The Appendix on pages 97–107 contains sample resumes and a resume-writing exercise for you to complete if you need to, as well as information on cover letters and interviewing skills.

SKILL	EXCELLENT	GOOD	POOR
Knowledge of co-op or internship opportunities			
Writing resumes			
Writing cover letters			
Interviewing techniques			
Knowledge of job-search resources on your campus			
Knowledge of job-search resources in your community			

Write down the skills you rated "good" or "poor," and indicate what you can do now to improve these skills.

SKILL	IMPROVEMENT ACTION

SUMMARY

In this unit you examined your alternative majors carefully in terms of your work values and other personal information. You have now made a commitment to a major and formed a graduation plan. You have also learned how this major relates to possible career directions.

Now that you have made a decision, you will need to complete the process by implementing that decision. Unit Six will help you establish a plan of action to accomplish this.

CASE STUDY: ROBERT

After a concentrated exploration process, Robert has decided on an education major in social studies. He has thought about being a teacher for some time, and all the personal, academic, and occupational information he has collected confirms this decision. He has also thought about entering law school some day since he thinks the field of educational law is a fascinating and important one. Robert has carefully organized a graduation plan to be his guide for the next two years. He is doing extremely well academically, so he has no doubt about his ability to complete his goal. He has looked at the job possibilities in education and is confident he will be able to find a position as a high-school social studies teacher after graduation. He has put together a tentative resume and intends to enlarge his scope of experience with children during the next two years.

What are Robert's next steps in order to implement this plan? What next steps do you need to take?

PERSONAL LOG #5

Summarize what you have learned from this unit and class discussions. How do you feel about making a commitment to a major? Have you ever made a commitment to an educational or career choice before? How is this decision different from past ones? How will you make future commitments?

_____

_____

_____

_____

_____

_____

_____

_____

_____

_____

_____

_____

_____

_____

_____

_____

_____

_____

_____

_____

_____

UNIT SIX
Implementing Your Decision

What the future has in store for you depends
largely on what you place in store for the future.

Anon

YOU ARE NOW READY to implement the decision you made in Unit Five and begin working with your new major. No decision is complete, however, until the first
step toward fulfilling it is taken. There are initial actions you need to take and goals
you need to set for future actions. Perhaps most important, you need to realize that no
decision is set in stone; decisions you make today can always be changed tomorrow.

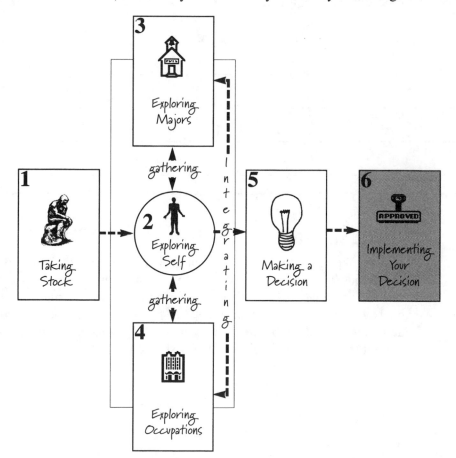

ACTION PLANNING

Now that you have chosen a major, you need to put your decision into action. The activities in this unit will assist you in implementing your decision in a satisfying and efficient way.

I have made a commitment to pursue the following major: _____

ACTIVITY: TAKING IMMEDIATE ACTION

There are several possible actions you can take to complete your decision. Check the action you intend to take now:

❏ Transfer to the department or college in my institution where my new major is located.

❏ Stay where I am until I can complete the requirements necessary to enter my new major.

❏ Enroll in another institution (e.g., university, community college, technical school).

❏ Stop my enrollment in college for a while.

❏ Other (please specify): _____

_____

_____

Whichever action you checked, you will need to take specific steps to accomplish that action. Break down the action into its component steps and write them here. (e.g., To enroll in my new major I will call my academic advisor to find out what procedures are required.)

1. _____

2. _____

3. _____

4. _____

5. _____

GOAL SETTING

As you take action to implement your decision, it is time to think about the future and the actions you will want to take now to prepare for when you leave college after graduation. This involves setting short- and long-term academic, career, and personal goals. In Unit One (p. 10) you wrote three goals you would like to accomplish by graduation. Review them before completing the following goal-setting activities to determine if they are still viable or if you wish to change them.

ACTIVITY: SETTING ACADEMIC GOALS

Now that you have outlined the action steps you need to take to implement your decision about a major, there are certain academic goals that you will want to set. Write your goals in specific, action-oriented terms. What do you need to do to make these goals come true?

Write a short-term *academic* **goal:** (e.g., Within the next two weeks I will sit down with my academic advisor and plan the coursework in my new major for each semester until graduation.)

_____

_____

_____

Steps I will take to implement this goal: (e.g., I will phone my advisor for an appointment today.)

_____

_____

_____

Write a long-term *academic* **goal:** (e.g., I will graduate with at least an A- average in all my major courses.)

_____

_____

_____

Steps I will take to implement this goal: (e.g., I will improve my study habits and spend more time preparing for each class.)

_____

_____

_____

ACTIVITY: SETTING CAREER GOALS

Although your academic goals are the most obvious part of fulfilling your commitment to your new major, thinking about your short- and long-term career goals is just as important as you progress toward your college degree. You might want to consider the work values that you chose on page 23 as you set your career and personal goals.

Write a short-term *career* **goal:** (e.g., I will put together a resume based on what I have accomplished up to now.)

_____

_____

Steps I will take to implement this goal: (e.g., I will visit the campus career planning office tomorrow to use their resume writing resources.)

_____

_____

Write a long-term *career* **goal:** (e.g., I will find a job after graduation that offers me personal satisfaction and has good prospects for my future.)

_____

_____

Steps I will take to implement this goal: (e.g., I will look into internship opportunities relating to my major and find out what is involved in taking part.)

_____

_____

_____

ACTIVITY: SETTING PERSONAL GOALS

Setting academic and career goals involves your personal needs and goals as well. Being successful in your academic and career life gives you personal confidence and satisfaction. Setting personal goals requires self-examination and reflection. What kind of person do you want to be when you graduate?

Write a short-term *personal* **goal:** (e.g., I will improve how I manage my time.)

_____

_____

Steps I will take to implement this goal: (e.g., I will sign up for a time management workshop that is offered at our campus counseling center.)

_____

_____

Write a long-term _personal_ **goal:** (e.g., By the time I graduate I will have taken advantage of the cultural and social opportunities offered on campus so that I can become a truly "educated person.")

_____

_____

Steps I will take to implement this goal: (e.g., I will check the campus newspaper every week to see what lectures, concerts, theater, etc. I might be interested in.)

_____

_____

Other academic, career, and personal goals I want to set:

_____

_____

_____

ACTIVITY: REEXAMINING PREVIOUS GOALS

In Unit One you wrote down some general goals you would like to accomplish by the day after graduation (p. 10).

Reexamine these goals to see if you would like to keep, change, or embellish them.

_____

_____

How are your present goals _similar_ to the previous goals you set?

_____

_____

How are your present goals _different_ from the previous goals you set?

_____

_____

Has the work you have completed in this course changed the way you view your academic goals? Career goals? Personal goals? If so, how?

_____

_____

_____

PERIODIC REASSESSMENT

Although you have chosen a major and set goals that seem satisfying and attainable, new information or events in your life may necessitate periodic reassessment of your decision. This is the nature of decision making. For instance, the coursework in your new major may not be as interesting as you thought it would be; your graduation plan may need adjustments after you take a few courses or begin your job search. Every decision is open to change and adjustment as you live with it.

There are no right or wrong decisions, just decisions that may or may not need to be altered down the road. Whether a decision is good or bad is based on how the decision is made, not on how the decision turns out. A good decision can, and often does, lead to a poor outcome, since external events that affect the decision are frequently beyond your control. This is why periodic reassessment of all your decisions is important.

SUMMARY

Congratulations! You have just completed the very important process of choosing a major. You have assessed your personal needs, gathered and analyzed information, and made a decision. You have now begun to take steps to implement your decision and set goals for the near and far future.

If you need to make adjustments later, you will be ready to make them. Remember that when you take control of the decision-making process, your chances of making choices that are personally satisfying and attainable are greatly enhanced.

CASE STUDY: YOU

Write a case study about yourself and how you explored various academic options and finally made a decision during this course (approximately 400 words or two double-spaced, typed pages). Describe how you felt at the beginning when you took stock of your situation. How did you feel as you gathered information about yourself, majors, and occupations? What aspects of that stage did you like the best? The least? How did you feel when you made a commitment to a major? What happened when you took the steps to implement that decision? How will you make educational and career decisions in the future?

_____

_____

_____

_____

_____

_____

_____

_____

_____

_____

_____

_____

_____

_____

_____

_____

_____

_____

_____

_____

Appendix

The Job Search: Resumes, Cover Letters, and Interview Preparation

ALTHOUGH YOU MAY THINK it is too soon to think about developing job search skills, career experts will tell you that preparing for a job after graduation should begin your first year in college.

In Unit Five, you visited a career services office to identify and explore jobs that interested you and that were related to your major. This is an important first step in preparing for a job search, but there are others, such as preparing a resume to inform potential employers of your qualifications, writing cover letters to accompany your resume or job application or to inquire about employment, developing your interviewing skills, and requesting letters of recommendation.

This appendix is intended only as a brief introduction to some of the job search skills you will need to acquire during your college years. You will have the opportunity to write a first-draft resume, learn what should be included in a cover letter, and review your skills as an interviewee. Your campus career services office probably has workshops or classes to help develop your proficiency in these and other aspects of the job search process. Remember, your campus career services office is a valuable resource to you in preparing for the work force. Don't wait until your senior year to make contact!

RESUMES

In completing the exercises in this workbook, you have had a chance to compile considerable information about yourself. Now is the time to organize this in the form of a resume for future use. A resume is a document that translates self-information into job-seeking terms. The resume introduces you to a potential employer and summarizes what you can offer. A good resume should:

- accurately portray your background
- emphasize your strengths
- be neat, complete, and concise
- have *no* spelling or grammatical errors

The two most common resume formats are the chronological and the functional. In order to determine which format will best represent your qualifications, consult with your instructor, check the Internet for examples, or review some of the resume publications that can be found in your library.

Chronological Format

The chronological resume is most familiar to employers. In it, jobs are listed in reverse chronological order, beginning with the most recent work experience and including information about the length of your employment, your employer, and the responsibilities and experience you gained on the job.

The main advantages of the chronological format are its familiarity to employers, the ease with which it can be prepared, and its ability to emphasize a steady work record. Its main disadvantage is its tendency to emphasize gaps in employment or lack of a well-developed employment history.

Functional Format

The functional resume ignores dates and employers and focuses instead on skills. It generally lists two or three skill areas to reflect the skills you gained in any and all previously held jobs, including any volunteer experiences.

The main advantages of the functional format are its emphasis on accomplishment and skill areas and its ability to camouflage a spotty or underdeveloped employment record. Its main disadvantage is that its structure may be more difficult to follow. In addition, the potential employer may want to know specifically where and when your identified skills were developed.

Sample Resumes

Now that you know more about how resumes are written, review the resume samples on the following pages. You will note that the difference in the two formats is only in Section III, Work History. Choose the format that will present your own experience most favorably and complete the appropriate resume draft exercise that follows the sample resumes.

JANE DOE

Current Address	Permanent Address
90 Sheldon Avenue	4240 Kodak Way
Oswego, NY 13126	Rochester, NY 14623
(124) 786-1234/jd.408@OSNY.edu	(222) 871-4321

CAREER OBJECTIVE

To obtain a position in a juvenile court system using my analytical, problem-solving, and research skills.

EDUCATION

State University of New York, Oswego, NY
Bachelor of Arts, Majors in Psychology and Criminology, 2004
GPA 3.3/4.0
Personally financed 100% of college expenses through employment and scholarships.

COURSE HIGHLIGHTS

Social Psychology	Constitutional Law
Adolescent Psychology	Law and Society
Psychology of Law	Spanish
Research Psychology	Social Work Law

SKILL AREAS

Interviewing

Advise students on academic, personal, and social matters in a campus residential setting. Make appropriate referrals.

Intern with a school psychologist and share responsibility for counseling/tutoring of high school students experiencing adjustment difficulties.

Screen and interview candidates being considered for resident adviser positions.

RESEARCH

Assist psychology faculty member with research design to assess and modify social environments.

Focus on classrooms, residence halls, and union facilities.

EMPLOYMENT HISTORY

Researcher, State University of New York (2002–present)

Intern, Oswego High School, Oswego, New York (2000–2001)

Resident Adviser, State University of New York (1999–2001)

Server, Mister Steak, Rochester, New York (summers)

REFERENCES

Available upon request.

JOHN DOE

Campus Address   Permanent Address
2222 Smith Hall   482 Cranberry Lane
Columbus, OH 43210   Berea, OH 44017
(614) 293-0000/jdoe.17@OSU.edu   (216) 243-4106

CAREER OBJECTIVE: To obtain an internship in accounting.

EDUCATION: **The Ohio State University,** Columbus, Ohio
Bachelor of Science, June 2004
Major in Accounting, Minor in Economics
Overall GPA: 3.0/4.0

WORK EXPERIENCE: **The Ohio State University,** Columbus, Ohio
(2001–2003)
Executive treasurer for a 450-resident dormitory. Prepared annual budgets, maintained a change fund, and was responsible for collection and disbursement of all monies. Implemented a new bookkeeping format, replacing the old one.

Stevens Management Company, Willoughby, Ohio
(summers of 2000, 2001)
Service manager assistant for newly developed condominium project. Responsible for contacting property contractors during construction and for resolving homeowner service requests as they occurred.

Daedallan Systems, Inc., Cleveland, Ohio
(summers of 1998, 1999)
Office assistant for independent service bureau. Tasks included data transmission, printing reports and customer statements, and preparing statements for mailing.

EXTRACURRICULAR ACTIVITIES: President, Student Accounting Association
Chair, Homecoming Weekend
Member, Economics Club, Men's Glee Club
Professional clown performer

REFERENCES: Available upon request

RESUME—FIRST DRAFT
Chronological Approach

Name: _____

Temporary Address: _____   Permanent Address: _____

_____   _____

_____   _____

Telephone: _____   Telephone: _____

I. Job Objective (or capsule resume)

In addition to naming the type of work you are seeking, try condensing your qualifications in a short statement at the start of your resume. For example: "Initial position in some phase of environmental control research. Laboratory skills. VISTA volunteer for three summers." or "Management trainee position in the banking industry involving supervisory and planning skills. Long-range goal is branch management."

_____

_____

_____

_____

_____

II. Education

Condense your educational qualifications here. Always put the most recent first.

_____

_____

_____

_____

_____

_____

_____

III. Work History

List each of your jobs, with the most recent first. Give dates of employment to account for all of your time, names of employers, titles of positions, and duties you performed in detail. Mention specific achievements in each job. Quantify if possible (e.g., supervised 10 staff members).

Dates	**Employers**	**Position Title and Duties**
_____	_____	_____
_____	_____	_____
_____	_____	_____
_____	_____	_____

IV. Honors

List any honors you have received or any honors activities in which you have been involved.

_____

_____

_____

_____

V. Activities and Interests

In the space below, highlight your professional and personal interests that would be of most interest to an employer.

_____

_____

_____

_____

VI. References

Write a statement that references are available upon request, or list the names, addresses, and phone numbers of two or three references that the employer can contact directly.

_____

_____

_____

RESUME—FIRST DRAFT

Functional Approach

Name: _____

Temporary Address: (Effective Dates) _____   Permanent Address: _____

_____   _____

Telephone: _____   Telephone: _____

E-mail address: _____

I. Job Objective (or capsule resume)

In addition to naming the type of work you are seeking, try condensing your qualifications in a short statement at the start of your resume. For example: "Initial position in some phase of environmental control research. Laboratory skills. VISTA volunteer for three summers." or "Management trainee position in the banking industry involving supervisory and planning skills. Long-range goal is branch management."

_____

_____

_____

_____

_____

_____

II. Education

Condense your educational qualifications here. Always put the most recent first.

_____

_____

_____

_____

_____

_____

_____

_____

III. Work History

List the skills and abilities you have developed or demonstrated. You do not need to associate one skill with one employer; you may have used one skill in several jobs.

Skills or Abilities	Job Titles and Responsibilities	Employers and Dates
_____	_____	_____
_____	_____	_____
_____	_____	_____
_____	_____	_____

IV. Honors

List any honors you have received or any honors activities in which you have been involved.

_____

_____

_____

_____

V. Activities and Interests

In the space below, highlight your professional and personal interests that would be of most interest to an employer.

_____

_____

_____

_____

VI. References

Write a statement that references are available upon request, or list the names, addresses, and phone numbers of two or three references that the employer can contact directly. (It is often recommended that this list be on a separate sheet.)

_____

_____

_____

COVER LETTERS

A resume should never be sent without a cover letter, which provides important information that is generally not included in the resume itself. The cover letter can personalize the application for the specific position.

The first paragraph usually identifies the position for which you are applying, may indicate where you heard about the position, and tells why you are interested in this particular position.

The second paragraph can add information about yourself that directly pertains to the specific position and reinforces important items in the resume itself. For example, you could briefly describe successful and relevant experiences that would benefit the prospective employer.

The last paragraph in a cover letter usually provides a phone number or an e-mail address where you can be reached and may inform the reader that you will be in contact to arrange a possible interview.

Cover letters are an important part of the job search process. They should always be addressed to a specific person by name and by title. Retain a copy of each letter in an organized job search file. A good cover letter and a well-developed resume are invaluable when your goal is to elicit a response that will lead to an interview.

SAMPLE COVER LETTER

90 Sheldon Avenue
Oswego, NY 13126

March 1, 2004

James A. Smith
Oswego County Juvenile Court
70 Spring Street
Oswego, NY 13111

Dear Mr. Smith:

My major professor at the State University of New York in Oswego, Dr. Lew Burns, has informed me of your recently posted position in the Juvenile Court system. As you can see from my enclosed resume, I will receive a degree in psychology and criminology in June. I am extremely interested in your position, and as a result of my education and experiences, I feel I bring strong qualifications for your consideration.

I have been involved in many paid and volunteer activities that have prepared me for work in the juvenile system. I interned with a public school psychologist during my junior and senior years and spent many hours in juvenile court working with offenders and observing how the system works. I have individually counseled several troubled youths and feel I had a positive impact on them. I also have strong research skills since I worked on several funded projects involving the etiology and behavior of juvenile offenders.

I would appreciate an opportunity to speak with you about the tasks involved in the position and to inform you in more detail about my expertise and qualifications. I will call you the week of March 4 to possibly set up an appointment. If you wish to reach me before then, please contact me at 444-6789 or jd.408@OSNY.edu. Thank you for considering me for an interview.

Sincerely,

Jane Doe

Jane Doe

INTERVIEW PREPARATION

Your careful preparation for interviews with recruiters or representatives from potential employers is extremely important. Job fairs or career days on your campus usually serve as a first screening. If you are well prepared for this first screening you will tremendously enhance your chances of being called for a second interview, usually held at the recruiter's offices.

You will want to learn as much as possible about the organization before interviewing with them. You should try to anticipate some of the questions you will be asked and have questions of your own prepared. The interviewer will be impressed if you can show that you have "done your homework" on the company and are able to ask intelligent questions about working there.

Your campus career services office should have information about any organizations that conduct on-campus interviews. Your library should have books and directories that list and describe many companies and organizations and that will give you some useful information. The most current information can usually be found on the organization's Web site. Sometimes you can find a recent story about an organization in the library's archived newspapers. And most important, remember to read and learn any materials you received from the interviewer at your first interview!

Some typical questions that interviewers will ask at either first or second interviews include:

- Tell me about yourself.
- Why are you qualified for this position?
- What are your long-range goals? Short-range goals?
- How do you expect to achieve these goals?
- What do you see yourself doing five years from now? Ten years?
- What was your major in college? Why did you choose it?
- What would be your ideal job?
- What do you know about this company?
- Will you relocate?
- Are you willing to spend six months as a trainee?
- How do you determine and evaluate success?